MW00596158

Praise for *Leadership Matters*

"As Publisher & Executive Editor of a dominant, global business digest, I've had the opportunity to review over 15,000 essays over the years, covering the entire business spectrum. Rarely do I come upon the level of truly authentic, cutting-edge thought leadership as discovered within this book. This isn't just a collection of anecdotal musings or rehashed wisdom, such as those mindlessly espoused by the current plethora of 'leadership consultants' hawking their latest revelations. What Len has expertly crafted and delivered here is a rare and priceless commodity these days—candid, actionable insights based on years of 'in the trenches' experience. In doing so, he dares to question timeworn, conventional thinking and theory in a refreshingly effective manner. For any forward-looking professional at any level of any organization seeking to truly 'break the mold' with intentional, authentic leadership action, this is the book (and indeed, the Bible) for you."

—Dennis J. Pitocco
Editor-in-Chief BIZCATALYST360.COM

"The unmistakable formula for Leadership Development is presented in here with surgical precision and in 'slow-release doses!' Len Bernat, the hands-on Leadership Architect, has unraveled the puzzle of all-around Personality Development with a precise plan of action. Written with the perspective of 'simple living and high-thinking,' this book deserves to be mandatory reading for all management students and aspirants."

—Bharat Mathur
best selling author of *You Are You-nique; Realize Your True Worth*

"In a world where leadership has become a buzzword devoid of true meaning, Len reminds us, *Leadership Matters.* His definition is clearly stated without jargon or gimmicks and serves as a practical guide, not only of what leadership means but also how to assume the mantle with ease and grace. Everyone who works with people, whether in management or aspiring to such, needs to read this book and embrace the lessons shared from Len's successful tenure as a true leader of people."

—Christine Andola
management consultant and published author

Leadership Matters

Leadership Matters

Len Bernat

Copyright © 2017—Len Bernat

ALL RIGHTS RESERVED—No part of this book may be reproduced in any form or by any electronic or mechanical means, including information storage and retrieval systems, without permission in writing from the authors, except by a reviewer who may quote brief passages in a review.

Published by Deeds Publishing in Athens, GA
www.deedspublishing.com

Printed in The United States of America

Library of Congress Cataloging-in-Publications data is available upon request.

ISBN 978-1-947309-19-7

Books are available in quantity for promotional or premium use. For information, email info@deedspublishing.com.

First Edition, 2017

10 9 8 7 6 5 4 3 2 1

To the wonderful leaders with whom I was privileged to serve in the Marine Corps—especially Rich Amano, Sam Flores, and Charles Ducharme. This book is a testimony to the wisdom, knowledge, and experience that helped a young man grow to his full potential as a leader of Marines. Semper Fi.

Introduction

I was lucky to spend 20 successful years in the United States Marine Corps where I began my career as private/recruit at Parris Island, South Carolina and ended my career as a Captain and leader of Marines at Meridian, Mississippi. I will be the first to tell you that the key to my success was not what I was able to accomplish on my own, but what I accomplished because outstanding leaders saw potential in me and forced me to grow in my technical skills and most importantly, as a leader.

So, when I entered the civilian job market, I expected that those in leadership positions would have the same high standards and love for leadership that I had experienced in the Corps. How could they not? Weren't there more books expounding the importance of good leadership and explaining what it took to be a good leader in the civilian world than I had ever seen in the military environment? But, sadly, I quickly realized that talking about leadership and actually being a leader did not necessarily go hand in hand. Let me give you some examples.

In my first civilian job, I was hired because I knew nothing about the product or the civilian manufacturing process. That sounds funny until you realized that this small plant had been bought out by a large corporation and upper-level management wanted to close the plant at which I was hired. Their logic was that I would be the perfect person to take an organization operating slightly in the red and nose dive it into such a losing operation that closing it could be justified as "good business" and not just a way to reduce competition. But they hired the wrong person. I quickly learned the process, engaged the workforce in improving the process, encouraged the team to work together toward success and soon, we were a profitable operation. My reward—I was laid off because of "too many upper-level managers" and the plant went back into the red under the new operating model. Within a few months, the plant was closed.

My next job was in retail at a building supply store. I was hired in a management position to oversee the plumbing, electrical, and cabinet departments. I studied the approved department layouts and carefully checked to ensure we were following the model. While on the floor, I engaged customers to try and find out what we could do to enhance their shopping experience. I soon discovered that we catered to a lot of "do it yourself" folks who knew what they needed but had a hard time finding it in our store. So, starting with the plumbing department, I changed the end caps (where you normally find sale items) to educational tools. One was a sink with all the plumbing that went under the sink—each part labeled with a number and a bin with the parts matching that number available so the customer could grab and go. I did the same for toilet installation/repair and water heater installation/repair. Soon, the president of the company was coming to pay a visit to find out why we were selling more plumbing parts than any other store in the chain. I proudly showed him the changes I made and to my surprise, I was instructed to dismantle my end caps and return them to the approved layout. When I explained that the new end caps were the reason for my sales increases, he did not care. He let me know that "the home office spent a lot of time figuring out how to layout a store for success and I had no right to change anything." My sales fell back in line with the rest of the stores and today, the chain no longer exists.

I helped a software company obtain a half-million-dollar contract only to see it go under due to the mismanagement of those funds. I helped a manufacturer take a successful business that had grown to $800,000 in annual sales to $2 million in annual sales in only one year, only to be told to look for another job because I was becoming too valuable to the operation. The owner then took his profits and closed the business because he no longer needed to work.

In every case, the downfall of the business came as a result of the leaders of the organization and not in the workforce. But the loser each time was the workforce who lost their jobs. So, I had to ask myself that one important question—why? Why would corporate leaders spend billions of dollars on leadership books and training and still end up 'killing the goose that lays the golden egg'?

It took me a while to realize that the answer to my question was the focus of the leaders. The leaders in the civilian environment were focused on preserving the corporate environment. They talked about people as if they were the most important part of the company's success. But clearly, their actions demonstrated

that preserving their sense of self-importance was more important. They talked about "thinking outside the box" but they hide
inside the box every time they came face to face with innovation
or success not brought about at their direction. Change, although
lauded as necessary for success, was discussed, however, it rarely
succeeded. (If you don't believe me, think about how many articles you have read about how to successfully implement change
in your organization.) So, closing a plant was more important
than appreciating the turn around that created a profit—keeping the uniformity of a retail layout was more important than
increased profit driven by customer satisfaction—spending profits faster than creating more revenue streams gave the feeling
of success—putting people out of work so you can enjoy your
monetary success trumps rewarding your team for making you
successful.

But in the military, our focus had to be the people. If we
were going to succeed in any mission, the ability of the people to
successfully function should the leader be killed was absolutely
necessary. So, the preservation of the organizational structure was
never important. The preservation of leadership—the ability for
someone to immediately step into a void created due to the harsh
realities of war—was our only guarantee to success. The eleven
principles of leadership were not just nice ideas—they were the
fundamental concepts by which we lived each day on active duty.
I benefited from people who invested time and energy into my
leadership development and I ensured that when I turned the
reigns of leadership over to the next generation of Marines, they
were ready to be the leaders of tomorrow.

If our economy is ever going to become as strong as it was before the Great Recession, corporate America has to change and refocus on people. The most amazing thing is that it really is a lot easier than the corporate world believes. So, I will take those eleven principles of leadership and the fourteen traits of an effective leader that I learned in the Marine Corps and share how I used them to create success stories. I know that some of the corrective actions I took can only be accomplished in a military environment where employment rules are very different. But the idea is not to provide you with instant solutions. My intent is to get you to think outside of the norm and not just solve problems, but be the kind of leader people will always follow.

Table of Contents

Part 1: Leadership Principles

1. Know Yourself

There is an old story I remember hearing long ago. A man decides he wants to change the world. As he sits down to consider the challenge, he realizes just how big the world is so he decides to narrow his focus. He would change the hemisphere in which he lives. No, that won't work because this is still too big of a challenge. So, he decides his focus should be changing his country — no, his state — no, his county — no, his town. Each time he realizes just how big the task would be. How about changing those who live on my street, he pondered, or just those who live in my house? Finally, he came to a solution. I will start my quest to change the world simply by learning what I need to do to change myself.

Entering into a leadership position can be a daunting challenge — there is so much to learn — so much to accomplish — so much riding on your success. The questions that keep you awake are the same for everyone — Where do I start? — How do I build trust with my new team? — Will I be able to meet the challenges that arise unexpectedly? — Will I be successful as a leader?

Rule number one for all leaders is this. **Know yourself and seek self-improvement.** You can't lead others if you do not know who you are as a person and what brought you to this point in your life. So many 'new leaders' make the mistake of imagining what they think a good leader looks like from past experience and acting in a manner that emulates this vision. The problem is that you will appear to be acting like a leader instead of being a leader. So, before taking on any new leadership challenge, take the time to get off by yourself and assess yourself. Make sure you write down your assessment — you are building your self-improvement plan and will need to know from where you are starting.

- Ask yourself, what are the strengths I know I possess that helped me get to this moment in life where I am about to be the leader of this new team? How can I use these strengths to begin the process of rallying my new team around my goals? How can these strengths bring value to the team? What can I do to improve my strengths so that I may be an exceptional leader?

- What are my weaknesses and how will these weaknesses create problems in my new leadership position. What can I do to overcome these weaknesses? Which weakness must be corrected immediately so I do not put the success of the team at risk? What tools are available to help me in my quest to improve myself?

- Finally, with your assessment in hand, you are ready for the hard part. Find a trusted friend who has known you for a long time or sit down with your boss who is putting you in the new position or if you are fortunate to have one, sit down with a trusted mentor and ask them to honestly tell you about your strengths and your weaknesses. Encourage them to be brutally honest. Compare what they tell you to your self-assessment but don't be too surprised if your lists do not match. And don't take it personally—if you honestly want to improve yourself, you have to be willing to let those you trust give you fair and honest feedback.

Let me share a personal example with you. I pastor a small church and have been their pastor for over 12 years. Each Sunday, I must stand before people I have grown to care for deeply and share with them insights from God's Word in hopes of helping them develop a close, personal relationship with our Heavenly Father. And each Sunday, I trust my wife to critique my message, my delivery technique, my strengths, and my weaknesses. Believe me when I tell you that sometimes it hurts—especially if I am really pleased with how I feel the message was delivered. But, I fight the urge to argue with her and I listen. Over the last 12 years, her honest feedback has made me a much better preacher and pastor. I need her to keep me grounded so that as the spiritual leader of our church, I serve God to the very best of my ability—being the vessel He uses to accomplish His purpose in the life of His children. My wife keeps me from becoming too focused on myself and constantly focused on my purpose for being a pastor. We all need this kind of honest feedback if we are going to excel in our leadership position.

Now that you have your assessment and the assessment of a trusted person in hand, you are ready to really work at your self-improvement plan. Here are some things you can do immediately to enhance your journey into leadership.

- Learn by studying the causes for success or the failures of other leaders. Two of my favorite leadership books are "The Art of War" by Sun Tse and "The Leadership Secrets of Attila the Hun" by Wess Roberts, Ph. D. You will have no problem finding excellent books to read. So, make your professional reading time a priority.

- Master the art of effective writing and speech. Take an effective writing course. Take a public speaking course. Join an organization like Toast Masters to hone your public speaking skills. Every leader will have to effectively communicate in both written and oral form. You must make communication skills a high priority if you are going to be an exceptional leader.

- Develop a genuine interest in people so that you can obtain an understanding of human nature. Remember, you are leading individuals who each have different passions, skills, abilities, backgrounds, education, etc. But somehow, someway, you, as the leader, must encourage them to work together to be successful. This is no small task but is the part of being a leader that is the most fun.

- Finally, have definite goals, a definite plan to attain each goal, and the ability to communicate this information to your team in such a way they want to help you get to the new destination because they are excited about the trip.

If you are looking for the foundation on which to build your leadership career, you now have it. As a leader, you will be encouraging your people to change, grow personally, and professionally help them be successful in their career—and you can only do that when you know how to change yourself.

2. Be Technically Proficient

I have been lucky in my lifetime to have met and worked with some wonderfully intelligent people. They are amazing people because every time I talked to them, through the stories they tell, the experiences they share, the lessons they impart, I would learn a new way of handling a problem, overcoming an obstacle or I would gain valuable professional knowledge. I would be like Mary sitting at the feet of Jesus and ignoring the hustle and bustle of Martha — not because what Martha was doing was not important but because what I was learning was so much more valuable.

In the first chapter, Know Yourself, I stressed the importance of knowing yourself and seeking self-improvement. As a leader, one of the important aspects of your leadership must be that you are technically proficient in your field of expertise. Not only must you **be technically proficient**, you also have an obligation to keep current of the latest innovations that are happening in your field, knowing the latest processes that are making advances in your field, and being at the cutting edge of setting the vision for where your field of expertise is evolving. In other words, you must be seen as a leader in your field. So here are some tips on what you can do to keep yourself prepared for the challenges of your leadership position.

- Seek continuing education programs that will keep you up-to-date on all aspects of your field. Utilize webinars, on-site training, subject matter training events, and conferences to obtain knowledge pertaining to the advances in your field and to reinforce lessons already learned. Additionally, seek opportunities to teach at these events. Nothing will help you more to increase your proficiency in a process than to have to do the research associated with preparing a well thought out and effective training session.

- Broaden your knowledge by being active in a professional organization associated with your field. You will be amazed at what you will learn and how you can help shape the future of your field of expertise by participating in these organizations. (I remember sitting in a meeting discussing how we were going to utilize desktop computers to manage supply assets in the Marine Corps in 1979. This was years before the first desktop computers had even been invented!)

- Seek out and associate with capable leaders. Observe and study their actions. As I mentioned in my opening paragraph, seek out those who teach you whenever you meet with them. And as you learn, share this knowledge with others—become the teacher.

- Seek opportunities to practice what you learn in your training session. As a procurement professional, I sent my buyer to a training session on how to write an effective Request for Proposals (RFP) and how to manage this important solicitation process. As soon as the buyer returned, I provided all the information I had on an RFP that needed to be written and told the buyer that this was her next assignment—I was available to answer questions but she would be completely responsible for the results. She was excited to take on the challenge because she would be able to practice what she had just learned.

- Finally, prepare yourself for the next higher job. Do not let yourself get complacent or become too comfortable in your position. You may never have the opportunity to move up to the next level of leadership, but if you are constantly preparing yourself for this opportunity, you will be amazed at how well you will be able to relate your day-to-day functions with the success of the organization. By understanding the big picture, you can contribute to the success of your organization by helping set the vision it needs to succeed tomorrow and each day into the future.

Let me close with an important caution. During the recent economic slowdown, I was so surprised that one area of "cost savings" that was instituted in so many organizations was the reduction of training dollars because of the travel expenses that go hand in hand. The unspoken message in this action was, "We want you to work harder because we are not going to replace people when they leave this organization, we want you to do more in the eight hours you are at work since overtime will not be allowed, we want you to work smarter so that you are using every tool provided in the most efficient manner, but we are not willing to invest in you as a person to help you succeed in these difficult economic times." Shame on leaders who embraced this philosophy! Never cut training.

Invest in yourself; invest in your people, invest in your organization; be technically proficient and succeed.

3. Seek Responsibility

I go way back with computers (a nice way of saying I am old). I remember keypunch cards. As a young Marine, I was there when the first aviation supply department conducted the very first wall-to-wall inventory using the computer-generated inventory aids — keypunch cards. As we were getting ready to start counting in the warehouse, a problem came to light. It seemed that some of our keypunch operators had been arrested at a party in town over the weekend and we now had to find someone to man the machines and that someone would be me. I let the Lieutenant know that I did not even know where the keypunch machines were located. He showed me and with help from the one available keypunch operator and the Sergeant in charge of our section, I was soon operating the machines like a pro.

I learned an important leadership trait that day without even realizing it. That is, as a leader, you have to **seek responsibility and take responsibility for your actions**. I can tell you that on the day that the Lieutenant took me to the keypunch office, I could tell by the tone of his voice that I had to succeed because his reputation was on the line. I was determined from that point on to succeed at this new task. Two weeks later, the inventory was finished on schedule, the inventory was considered a big success, the lessons learned were shared with other aviation supply departments, and I was officially on my way to becoming a keypunch operator, having demonstrated the proficiency needed to be assigned this field as a secondary Military Occupational Specialty (MOS). I had met the responsibility head on knowing my actions would determine the results.

So, if you are going to be a responsible leader, here are some things that will be important to your development toward this goal.

- I said this before and I will say it again. Learn the duties of your immediate senior so that should the opportunity arise, you will be able to move up into that position. If you never get the opportunity, you will at least have a better understanding of the organizational structure and how your functions contribute to the success of your organization.

- Seek different leadership positions that will give you experience in accepting responsibility in different fields. This can be done at work or in a volunteer capacity. So, join the Chamber of Commerce and work on one of their committees with the intention to someday lead that committee. Volunteer at your local church in a behind the scenes role that is matched with your natural talents. Find a non-profit that touches your heart and give freely of your time to help them in events. Opportunities to lead abound!

- When given an opportunity, take it. You may think that it is outside your comfort zone or beyond your capabilities but you will be surprised at how successful you can be when you muster the courage to take the chance. So, if your boss asks you to head up a special project, don't be afraid to say yes.

- Perform every act, large or small, to the best of your ability. When you accept a responsibility, it is your chance to shine — so shine. Your reward will be increased opportunities to perform bigger and more important tasks in the future because you will be seen as the kind of person who always gives their very best effort to make a team successful.

- In the absence of clear instructions, take the initiative to perform actions you believe the person who placed you in this position of responsibility would direct you to perform if he/she were present. Remember, your goal is to be successful, not to elevate yourself by making your boss look bad.

- Should one of your team members not perform up to your expectations, carefully evaluate their failure before taking action. Make sure you did not contribute to their apparent shortcomings. Ask yourself if your instructions were clear, were the proper tools provided in a timely manner, did you follow up to see if the person was on task. Always look at a team member's poor performance as a way to evaluate and learn new ways to improve your leadership. And if the failure is because the team member did not perform their task properly, then provide them with constructive feedback and corrective action. Remember, you may have to work with this person again in the future and would like better results, not resentment.

- Finally, and this may be the most important tip I share with you, stand up for what you think is right. You must have the courage of your convictions because, in the end, the one person you must confront every day of your life is you. I once was asked to do something I knew was illegal. When I refused, I was warned that my behavior would make me appear like I was not a team player. My response was simple. If this is a team building exercise, send me an email asking me to take the action and I will be glad to do so since it will be under your authority. Of course, the response was, "I can't do that!" Mine was, "Then you did not ask." See, I know that each morning, I have to look at myself when I wash my face, shave, and brush my teeth and I wanted to like who was looking back at me. If I were to lose my integrity, my honor, my sense of self, then I would never like the image I see in the mirror.

So that you know how important this is to me, let me share a final story with you. When Hazel and I entered the realm of the empty-nester, we got a puppy. Our youngest daughter came by to meet little Norm and was playing on the floor with him. I heard her say, "So, Norm, if you are going to live in this house, you have got to be responsible. If you pee on the floor and get your nose rubbed in it, it is your fault—you are totally responsible for your own actions and the results." I laughed and she looked up in horror that I had heard her say what she did to the dog. But I could not help telling her, "Well, I know now that you were listening." I am proud of the responsible young woman she has become.

Be responsible for your actions and succeed.

4. Make Sound and Timely Decisions

After a rather severe ice storm, the Fire Chief came to my office with a handful of paperwork. He explained that during the storm, the Fire Departments realized they did not have enough chain saws to get all the fallen trees cut up and moved out of the road-ways to ensure emergency equipment could continue to be available to our citizens. He knew he should have gotten a Purchase Order prior to obtaining the chain saws, extra blades, and small engine oil but he just wanted to get his crews out doing what was necessary to open-up the roadways. Therefore, he went to a hardware store where the County had an account and just charged them to that account. I took the paperwork and told him I would sort through it and prepare the necessary paperwork to get the approval from the Chairman of the Board of Commissioners and that he should not worry. He needed to make a decision for the good of the people and my job was now to support his decision.

The Fire Chief demonstrated a very important leadership trait. Every leader will be faced with situations and problems that require the leader to react. As a leader, we must learn to **make sound and timely decisions.**

So, if you are going to be an exceptional leader, you must be prepared to make decisions. That means you have to develop the skills that are necessary to prepare you for that moment of truth when the chips are down and you must rally your team to success. Here are some things you can do to help you develop the kind of decision-making skills that lead to success.

- Develop a logical and orderly thought process. Every process consists of a first step, the last step, and many steps in between. Therefore, being able to logically outline each step that must be accomplished to obtain the final goal will be invaluable in developing a plan to fulfill the goal. This skill is so important to the decision-making process that you should practice outlining objectives for different and difficult situations and prepare step by step solutions just to sharpen this skill. The time spent in these drills will pay dividends.

- When time and the situation permits, plan for every possible event that can reasonably be foreseen. Clearly define the final objective and goals that must be accomplished to consider the project completed successfully. With the goal in mind, use the above process to outline each step that must be accomplished to meet the goal. Once you know the steps you need to take to get to your goal, then you can evaluate the obstacles that may arise that can hinder your forward process. In this manner, you will be prepared to overcome each obstacle. You cannot over plan. But be aware of a pitfall that can come with the planning of a project. Do not get so bogged down in the planning process that you never move forward.

- Encourage your team to make plans at the same time you do if time is available. In this manner, your first meeting to begin the process of finalizing the plan will be more productive since the team is already prepared to discuss their ideas.

- Consider the advice and suggestions of your team members whenever possible before making the final decisions. Since it will normally take a team effort to meet most goals, then the team should be part of the planning process. This will allow you to tap into one of your most important resources — the skills and logic of the folks who will be working with you to meet the goal. If you want them on board, bring them into the process and allow their ideas to be heard and implemented when they add value to the plan. By taking this step, the goal is no longer just yours — it becomes the team's goal.

- Announce decisions in time to allow your team members to prepare for success. Once you have a plan, each member of the team may have to make adjustments to their schedules to help with the project. They may need to do some research or obtain material to execute their portion of the project. They may need to coordinate efforts with another department or agency outside of your office. Give them as much time as possible to ensure they can create their own plans and that they can feel successful. And of course, follow up with them so that you can ensure everyone is heading toward the objective.

- Make sure your employees are familiar with corporate level policies and plans. As with any project, there may be corporate policies and objectives that must be taken into consideration when formulating the process by which the project will proceed. If your employees are familiar with these policies, then the planning will ensure the project follows these guidelines.

- Consider the effects of your decisions on all members of your team. We all have that 'go to' person in our organization; that individual who seems to be able to accomplish any task that we place on them. But if we are not careful, this one person soon becomes overwhelmed by the extra workload. Learn to develop all team members equally so that projects are spread over the entire organization and not always given to the same person or persons. Remember, a successful project is one of the surest ways to move your team from good to exceptional.

- Finally, not all situations will afford you the opportunity to accomplish the steps outlined above. Sometimes, you have to quickly evaluate an emergency situation and formulate a quick solution to protect others. The more you practice the above steps, the better prepared you will be for the emergency. So, when this happens, make a decision based upon past experiences. In most cases, you will be right—but in every case, making a decision will be better than doing nothing.

I remember as a new warrant officer in the Marine Corps, one of my trusted senior enlisted computer operators told me that I was headed for trouble because I was willing to make decisions and then move to implement the decision quickly. I smiled and let him know that in my opinion, that was what I was being paid to do and until told otherwise, that was what I intended to do. When he asked me why I was willing to stick my neck out like that, I told him that I had worked for too many people who were in positions of leadership but could not make a simple decision for fear it might be wrong. I hated working for indecisive people and I swore to myself that once I earned a leadership role, I would never subject my people to wishy-washy decision making. I would rather be wrong than do nothing at all.

Be the leader—learn how to make wise decisions in a timely manner.

5. Set the Example

In 1987, during the war between Iraq and Iran, the Iranians started dropping mines into the waters of the Persian Gulf. The American response was to direct the USS Guadalcanal from the Mediterranean Sea to the Gulf with the Navy mine sweeping helicopters on board. Our mission was to lead the oil tankers and supply ships through the Gulf so that the mines would be found before any of the ships would hit them. I was on the USS Guadalcanal as the Aviation Supply Officer with the deployed Marines helicopter squadron. A small contingency of Marines and helicopters would go to the Gulf as part of the Special Task Force deployed for this dangerous mission. When we arrived at the port in Bahrain to obtain our assessment brief, one of the oil tankers that had hit a mine was sitting in full view—a big hole in the front of the ship demonstrated the threat we were facing. Upon setting sail, I met with my team comprised of Marines, sailors from the mine sweeping squadron, and sailors assigned to the ship's company. The first question they wanted to know was if we hit a mine, where would it explode. Since our office spaces were in the nose of the ship, I knew they had seen the damage to the oil tanker and they knew, as I knew, that our work spaces were in the blast area. I had to find a way to assure them that we needed to focus on our mission and not on the "what ifs." My solution was simple.

"Gentlemen, I saw the oil tanker and the damage to the front of the ship. I will not lie to you and say our spaces are not at risk." I began. "But, I can also assure you that the Navy/Marine Corps team on board this vessel constitutes the finest mine sweeping capabilities in the free world today. Therefore, to prove to you I have no fear that our team will find a mine before our ship can hit one, I will remain in our workspaces from this moment on until you all decide I can resume a normal schedule. That means I will only leave these spaces for required meetings, to use the head (bathroom for civilians), and retrieve my meals which I will eat right here at my desk. I will live in these spaces, day and night, until you decide I can leave. Any questions?"

As you can imagine, they did not expect this as my answer to their question. So, for two full days, I lived in the spaces. Finally, on day three, as we met for our nightly turnover meeting, they all agreed that I had proven my point and I could resume a normal routine. I then looked at them and told them this simple truth, "You have seen just how dedicated I am to you. Now let me say this. Should we hit a mine and our spaces are damaged, if you survive, do not give up. I am coming to get you. As I demonstrated, nothing, and I mean nothing, will keep me from protecting my people. You must hang on — I will be there!"

I am proud that each Marine and sailor was able to go home safe and sound to their loved ones. And hopefully, they learned the importance of setting a good example for their people. If you are going to be a leader that people will follow, **set the example** of what you expect. Here are some things you should always remember.

- Show your employees that you are willing to do the same thing you ask of them. I walk around my current workspace and every time I see trash on the floor or something out of place, I stop and fix it. I don't call for the cleaning person — I am more than capable of picking up trash. It is a little thing, but it says we are all responsible for our work space.

- Be professional in your personal appearance. Wear your work attire with pride. Ensure your appearance matches your level of leadership. There is some truth in the saying "dress for success" so do it. Your people will quickly see that you value a professional appearance and will want to follow your lead.

- Maintain an optimistic outlook. The more difficult the situation is, the better your chance to display an attitude of calmness and confidence. This is why I was willing to sit at my desk for as long as it took to get my team to know I would keep them safe in the Gulf. By showing confidence in our Navy/ Marine Corps team, they overcame their fear of the unknown.

- Conduct yourself so that your personal habits are not open to criticism. Your moral and ethical behavior are important. Always remember that what you say is not as important as what you do. If your actions do not match your words, you will quickly lose the respect of your team.

- Exercise, initiate and promote the spirit of initiative in your employees. I have become the point of contact for anything that falls outside the norm because, as I heard, "That's why I call Len. He finds a way to fix the problem." My hope is that my example will be seen and emulated by those around me.

- Avoid showing favoritism to any member of your team. Showing favoritism to one person on your team is the quickest way to begin the process of losing the respect of your team members. You do not have a favorite child — don't have a favorite team member.

- By your performance, people should know that you are the best person for the position you hold. When someone asks you how you got your job, the look on their face should indicate that they wish to know about your experience, how you heard about the job, the application and the interview process. You do not want them to be looking at you like you have two heads and that they are pretty sure you must be related to the owner because they would never hire someone like you. Be professional at all times.

- Delegate authority and avoid over-supervision in order to develop leadership among your team. I once worked for a small company where the owner had to approve every decision being made. Unfortunately, he did not make himself readily available to the staff to enable them to get the necessary guidance and approval. So, deadlines were never met and on some days, nothing could be accomplished because no one had the approval to move forward. The company went under and the owner blamed the staff and not the fact he was the obstacle to success.

Finally, let me close with part two of from the mine sweeping mission. As we turned over the mine sweeping helicopters to the USS Okinawa when our time on station was completed, the Aviation Storekeeper First Class Petty Officer from the mine sweepers transferred to the new ship in the first wave of people. He did so because I wanted him to make sure he inspected the working spaces, sleeping spaces, and mess decks so he could make sure his people had the essentials upon arrival. Just before our ship set sail for home, I heard an announcement over the ship's intercom — the captain of the ship was letting everyone know that a helicopter was about to land and my division needed to get them the part they needed as quickly as possible so we could set sail for home. I staged my people ready to meet the demand as quickly as possible. When I saw the Petty Officer casually walking toward our space, I asked him what he needed and he said he had to speak to me. Here is what he said. "Lieutenant, I have spent 11 years in the Navy. In the four months I have served with you, I have learned more about my job and about leadership than in all the previous years. I just could not leave without saying thank you."

I was amazed and said, "Are you telling me you held up a United States war fighting ship just to say thank you?"

"Yes," he stammered almost afraid to answer.

"Cool," I responded with a smile. "Now let's get you an empty box and wrap it up so it looks like you actually needed a part and you don't end up in trouble." With that, I sent him on his way to lead his team.

If you are going to change the life of those around you, remember, they will be watching you. **Set the example**.

6. Know Your People

While conducting leadership training with my second lieutenants in the Marine Corps, I posed this question to them from a real-life experience.

You have a Sergeant working for you who does an outstanding job every day. You have never had a problem with him or his work. One day, you notice that he just could not do anything right. How would you go about getting the Sergeant back in the game?

The answers ranged from "take him aside and chew him out" to "formally counsel him" and the ever popular "nothing—we all have bad days." I then told them how I handled this situation.

I asked the Sergeant to get a cup of coffee and follow me outside. Once outside I said, "I noticed you are having a hard time concentrating today. I can tell something is bothering you. What's going on, Sergeant, and how can I help?" The Sergeant told me that he had to take his wife to the emergency room the night before and they had admitted her with pneumonia. He barely got into work on time because he had to get his son off to school after being awake all night with him at the hospital. He had no idea how he was going to get him after school. I told him to go home and take care of his family. To call in each morning after he got his son off to school so that I knew he was okay and then go sit with his wife until they released her from the hospital. Once she was home, get her back on her feet before you come back to work. I told him I would take care of informing everyone else that needed to know.

I then looked at my lieutenants and asked, "How come no one thought to ask the Sergeant what was wrong?"

When you have been entrusted with the leadership of a team of individuals, you have an obligation to **know your people and to look out for their welfare**. Now, admittedly, the solution offered in the above example is something that can only happen in the military environment, but we do have ways to ensure we can take care of our team members when they need our support the most. So, here are some things to keep in mind.

- Put your employees' welfare before your own. I remember my first year at Jackson County that our interim County Manager had all the folks on the top floor of our office leave at noon on the day before our Christmas break. The payroll clerk said they would have to take vacation time for the time off and he informed her that he would personally sign the payroll adjustments so they would be paid. When the receptionist stated she would have to stay and answer the phone, he told her to show him how to work the switchboard phone and he would sit there all afternoon and take care of incoming calls. When she protested, he said, "Don't worry. Len will stay here to keep me company and see to it I do your job correctly." I enjoyed the afternoon of his story telling and they enjoyed time with their families.

- Correct grievances and remove discontent as quickly as possible. Nothing will create discord faster than allowing personnel problems to fester. If someone behaves in a manner that violates established policies, correct it. If someone is a gossip, correct it. If someone is not carrying their share of the workload and others constantly have to take up the slack, correct it. Be fair but be quick about resolving personnel issues before they explode and you have someone filing a formal grievance. Once that happens, then you are the problem.

- Make sure that you see your employees every day. Stop by their office or cubical, engage them at the coffee pot or copier, invite them into your office but always be approachable and available to talk to them. If possible, create a nice sitting area in your office with a table and two comfortable chairs so that you can sit in a position of equality with your employees and not in the dominant "behind the desk" position.

- Get to know and understand your employees. If they have special interests outside of work, asking about that interest will open the door to conversation. In this manner, if there are problems in the air, they will be willing to be open and honest with you about what is bothering them. They will also be willing to share ideas and thoughts with you that may lead to process improvements that will benefit the entire team. Open communications are vital to team building. But you must be absolutely sincere about your interest. Nothing will hurt your communications with your team faster than faking your interest in their personal life.

- Let them see that you are dedicated to their success. I had the privilege of working with a very motivated intern recently. On the days that he worked and before he left for the day, he would ask me to give him a leadership lesson. I would pose a question and let him answer and then share my experience with him. It was so enjoyable to see him grow because toward the end of his internship, he was coming up with really good solutions to complex problems. On his last day, I gave him my business card and told him that when he needed a reference, I would be honored to recommend him. When he called, I asked him one simple question, "Do you really want this job?" When he said yes, I knew I could get it for him and he works there today.

- Help your employees get the support from available personnel services. I opened up with an example of how I helped one of my Marines during a crisis in his life. I did what I knew I could legally do to help him. You should know all the programs your company has to help employees in their time of need. If you don't know what is available, visit your Human Resource office and start educating yourself today. Get to know what charitable organizations in your area are available to help should your employee need assistance that is outside the realm of your employee assistance programs. Always remember, it is your responsibility to care for your employees so don't just pass the employee off to HR and expect them to handle your responsibility.

- Ensure fair and equal distribution of rewards. Employee of the Month, Employee of the Year, and Certificates of Appreciation are designed to motivate your team but can quickly create problems if the same person is always in receipt of these awards. It is your responsibility as the leader to ensure each team member grows so they are eligible for these special recognition awards. But never forget, a "thank you" or a "good job" spoken in front of their peers is priceless and should be handed out sincerely and freely.

- Finally, encourage individual development. Give your team every opportunity to attend training, participate in webinars, conduct in-house training, or go to school after hours. When they raise a question, take the time to give them the big picture answer (i.e. the who, what, where, when and why the answer you are about to give is correct under the current situation so that they understand the logic and motivation behind the answer) and not just a quick yes or no. If you want them to be successful while on your team, make sure they have the tool of knowledge that will ensure their success.

I once had a veteran working for me who was suffering silently with Post Traumatic Stress Disorder (PTSD). When the "whispers" made their way to my ears, I invited him into my office for a cup of coffee. Slowly, I began peeling the layers of his defenses until he admitted just how bad he was suffering. He wanted help but just did not know what to do and feared that if he admitted the problem, he would lose his job. I sent him back to work and told him I would get with him later that day. I called a contact I knew at the Veteran's Administration and found out that there was a group of veterans with the same problem meeting in our area but that he would have to call them himself. They were very protective of their group since people with PTSD were often misunderstood and they would ensure this was a person with a real problem and not someone looking for headlines. I provided the information to my employee and told him it was now up to him to help himself—he had to make the call. Later, after he had attended several meetings, he thanked me for caring enough to help him find this group. He now knows that he was not alone and that he will be able to overcome the fear in time.

If you want to be an **exceptional leader**, get to know your team.

7. Develop a Sense of Responsibility Among Your Employees

"Top (an affectionate term we used for a Master Sergeant in the Marine Corps), I have noticed something disturbing. We have three Sergeants assigned to us but only one of them actually works. Two are willing to watch the third work and I find this unacceptable. You have one week to get this situation turned around or I will."

As a Marine Captain in charge of a section in the Aviation Supply Department, I had noticed something that should have been evident to all but no one wanted to address. I was not about to join those who turned a blind eye. (By the way, the solution I used could not be used in the civilian work environment; I understand that this is the case. However, since the rules in the military are different, I could be creative with my solutions. Therefore, I provide this story as a way for the reader to consider innovative solutions to leadership problems.)

A week later, I approached the Master Sergeant, "Top, you have not addressed the problem with the two Sergeants not carrying their load. I am assuming you told them they needed to work harder, right?" A nod of the head let me know I was on the right path. "So, now, I will fix it. Round up the three Sergeants and join me in my office."

Once they were assembled, I began by addressing my two problem children, "I assume the Top told you two that I am not happy with your performance and told you that you needed to work harder. Am I correct?"

"Yes, Sir."

"The problem is that there is no way we can measure 'work harder' is there?" I continued, "If I tell you that I feel you are not working harder, you can easily reply that you truly are which may or may not be true — but I just have no way of telling. So, I need to come up with a solution that will solve my problem in a way that I can measure the improvement."

I looked at the Sergeant who was carrying the work load, "What time do you get here each morning and what time to you leave each night?"

He replied, "I get here at six each morning and stay until about eight each night."

"Do you go to lunch each day?" I asked.

"No, Sir."

"Okay," now the fun was about to begin as I addressed the other two Sergeants, "you two have new working hours. Each day, you will be here five minutes before him so tomorrow morning you will be here by 5:55 am. You will not leave each night until five minutes after him so tonight you will be here until 8:05 pm. And if he does not go to lunch, you will not go to lunch. Now, this I can measure. So, if you want to go back to normal hours, you need to roll up your sleeves and start working together as a team. That way all of you can come in at the normal time each morning, all of you can go to lunch, and all of you can leave at the end of the normal work day. But it is completely in your hands. Your hours will continue in this manner until I am satisfied you are now a team. Top, make this happen and ensure the night shifts and mid shifts document the arrival and departure of these two. Dismissed."

I can tell you that in a very short period of time, they were working normal hours as a team.

As a leader, you must make sure that your team understands that the success or failure of the entire team is the responsibility of each member of your team. If any one person does not take their responsibilities seriously, then the entire team suffers and you, as the leader, are totally responsible. So, to **develop a sense of responsibility among your employees**, remember these important aspects of your leadership.

- Tell your employees what to do, not how to do it. Let them figure out the best way they can accomplish each task since they will know what works for them.

- You should then hold them responsible for the results they produce but you must never forget that the overall responsibility for getting the job done rests with you.

- Delegate enough authority to your employees to enable them to accomplish each task. Nothing is more frustrating to your employees than to not have the ability to make a decision that will enable them to quickly accomplish a task. You hired an adult so treat them like one and give them the authority they need to be successful.

- Give your employees frequent opportunities to perform duties usually performed by the next higher person. This will help them understand how their responsibilities fit into the overall operation and will help them prepare for advancement should an opening become available. Cross training is critical to success. Of course, when they are successful at meeting these duties, be sure to recognize their creativity, initiative, and a job that was done well.

- Correct errors in judgment and initiative in a way which will encourage the employee to try harder. Remember that honest errors should be acceptable because we learn from our mistakes and failures. So, outline what was done wrong, why it was not a good decision, how to reach a good decision should the circumstance arise again, and define what would have been the proper decision to make. Make every opportunity to provide correction a learning experience and not just an opportunity to exert your authority as the boss. And remember the adage, praise in public, criticize in private. You do not want to embarrass a team member in front of their peers.

- Give advice and assistance freely when it is requested by your team but do not do it for them. Help them to learn and grow so that they are empowered to succeed.

- Never, and I repeat because it bears repeating, never micro-manage. It will destroy initiative, drive, innovation, and enthusiasm. It will create boredom and increase the workload on the more seasoned employees because everyone will be afraid to make decisions out of a fear of the consequences.

- Assign your employees to positions in accordance with demonstrated or potential ability. For example, if you notice an employee is constantly helping others, they would be a good candidate for providing training for your team during your local training sessions.

- Be prompt and fair in backing your employees. Until convinced otherwise, have faith in each one of them and their judgment.

- Finally, as the leader, accept responsibility willingly and insist that your team live by the same standard.

I remember when I worked at a family owned building materials retail store that I noticed that one of the cashiers was always finding ways to improve the appearance of her station when she had no customers to check out. When I needed a department head for my plumbing department, I approached her to discuss giving her the position. She was hesitant because she knew very little about plumbing. But I assured her I could teach her the basics she would need to be able to talk to customers and I walked her through the department pointing out what could be done to really make it so much more customer friendly. I stressed that it would be her department, her chance to grow, her chance to challenge herself, and her chance to shine. She accepted the responsibility and promised she would give her best. She did an amazing job and became a trusted adviser to many of the other department heads because of her success.

The time you spend developing your team's **sense of responsibility** will help you create a dynamic force that will be committed to the success of all members of the team. This kind of **exceptional leadership** pays huge benefits because your people encourage each other, help each other, and ensure each team member shines.

8. Keep Your Employees Informed

I normally try to share positive examples of leadership with you when I write because I want to encourage you to think about leadership as a way to help your employees grow. However, I have found that sometimes, examining leadership failures that should never be repeated can leave a lasting impression. So, I apologize up front because you should be appalled by the true story I am about to share with you.

A county government was faced with a difficult challenge. The economic downturn had greatly reduced revenues and it became evident that it was going to be necessary to execute a reduction in force (RIF). Since there were not many employees getting ready to retire, the reduction was going to require that some employees would have to be laid off. The County Manager, Finance Director, and Human Resources Director began to meet behind closed doors to select the names of the people who would be laid off. No department heads were consulted, cuts would be made "equally" in all departments without considering actual work load, and no one was told that a RIF was being formulated. Once the list of employees to be laid off was completed, the Information Technology Department Head was told that on a specific date and

43

time, the log on information for the 44 employees being released would be disabled so that after they were told, they could not go back to their desks and get on their computers. Invitations were sent to the 44 employees for a special presentation so that when they walked in, they had no idea what they were about to face. Image what it must have been like to suddenly hear that you were being laid off effective immediately and that the unemployment office people were available to help them complete the forms for signing up for unemployment. If a RIF could be handled with less compassion, I do not know how.

It does not matter how difficult the news is, as a leader you have an obligation to **keep your employees informed** concerning what is going on in the organization. I remember being told I would be laid off from my very first job I had after retiring from the Marine Corps on the day I was closing on the purchase of my new home, so I could empathize with employees in the above example. Let me share some good ways that you can keep your employees informed.

- Whenever possible, explain why tasks must be done and how the task relates to the success of a project or the organization's overall mission. This really does not take an inordinate amount of time but pays such big benefits. Remember, unless it is a life or death situation, your employees should never be treated like children so the answer, "Because I said so," is never the right answer to their question of "Why?"

- Assure yourself that immediate subordinates are passing on necessary information. If it is important for you to take the time necessary for you to provide your team leaders information on the "who, what, where, when, and how," then you need to ensure they pass this information on to their team members. When you expect the information to be passed down, tell your team leaders that is what you expect them to do. It is really that simple to ensure everyone is kept informed. By keeping everyone up-to-date and fully involved in the process, you will contribute to the success of the project.

- Be alert to detect the spread of rumors. Rumors can harm your organization and can create problems that affect morale, performance, motivation, and trust. Once you are aware that rumors are being spread, replace the rumors with the truth immediately. Never allow rumors to flourish.

- Build morale by publicizing information concerning successes in your unit. Post awards earned by the team in a place of prominence so that even visitors can view your successes. If your organization recognizes longevity milestones such as five-years of employment, ten-years of employment, etc., ensure pictures are taken of your employee receiving the award and display it in the break areas for others to see. When you receive letters of thanks from customers or clients, gather your team and read the letter to them and then display it for all to see that your efforts produce positive results. Most importantly, always gather the team together after the completion of a project and thank them for their dedication and hard work.

Let them know you recognize that the success of the organization comes from its most valuable asset—the people.

- Hold after action meetings with your team after the completion of a project to discuss what went right and what went wrong. Discuss solutions to problems (but do not allow folks to begin blaming each other for problems) and discuss how to capitalize on the successes of a project.

- Keep your people informed about current decisions affecting their pay, promotion, privileges, and other benefits. These areas have a direct impact on the employee and their family so these are the things that will keep them awake at night. If you want your employees to truly believe that your concern for their welfare is at the forefront of your leadership, then keeping them up-to-date on the decisions being made that affect these areas and your efforts to impact those decisions are critical to their well-being.

Let me give you an example of a better way to manage the difficult news of a lay off so you can see how you can turn a negative into a positive. While working at a building supply retail store, the President of the company insisted that we had too many cashiers and demanded I lay off the last cashier hired by the end of the day. I tried to explain to him that the person he was talking about was an outstanding worker and that one of my other cashiers was getting ready to graduate from college and would most likely be leaving which would bring me in line with his desire. He would not listen and I was forced to lay off the cashier that day.

My first action was to begin calling on all the retail establishments around my location. Sure enough, I found a large chain store that was advertising for cashiers so I asked to speak to the person who would be responsible for hiring for the positions. Once I had her on the phone, I explained my problem and asked her if she could help me out by hiring this person I was to lay off that very day—I would send her over to the store within the hour if she would guarantee me that she would hire my cashier. She was amazed that I would do such a thing and promised that the job was hers if she came by that day and filled out the application.

I then asked the cashier to join me in the personnel office and explained to her that we had to cut her position due to downsizing decisions that were a must for the survival of the store. I then was able to tell her that I had arranged for her to be hired at the store across the street so that she would not be hurt by the layoff and that whether she stayed with the new assignment or not, it would help her financially until she decided what would be best for her. I gave her the manager's name she should ask to see and my business card so the manager would know I was the person sending her. A week later I purposely went to the store just to ensure she was working and happy with her new situation. She was grateful that I took the time to help her and explain to her that all was not lost during a difficult transition in your life.

Be an exemplary leader—communicate with your peo-

ple—let them know what is going on—make them feel important to the team and to you.

9. Ensure Assigned Tasks Are Understood, Supervised, and Accomplished

I watched a fellow Marine Captain embarrass himself by of issuing a very clear and concise order without thinking of the consequences behind the order. He set up a desk and chair in our warehouse and told a Gunnery Sergeant he was not very fond of to sit there every day and do absolutely nothing because everything he did was wrong. The Captain then wrote a fitness report (the civilian equivalent would be a performance evaluation) and graded him as "unsatisfactory" in the area of regular duties among other very low grades. Then the Captain proceeded to process the Gunnery Sergeant for an administrative discharge on the grounds of incompetence. The Gunnery Sergeant was afforded a military lawyer to represent him during the formal proceedings and the questioning of the Captain went something like this.

"So, let me make this clear so that all can understand. You ordered the Gunnery Sergeant to sit at the desk in the warehouse you had set up for him and do nothing. Is that correct?"

"Yes."

"And what did he do?"

"He sat there and did nothing," replied the Captain with indignation in his tone.

"So, he followed your order completely and did exactly what you told him to do. Therefore, when I look at this fitness report and see that you marked him unsatisfactory in the area of regular duties that would be a lie because his very act of sitting there and doing nothing, by your own admission, was fulfilling his assigned duties completely. As a matter of fact, by your own statement, he was outstanding at sitting there and doing nothing. Is that not correct?"

"Well, no," the startled Captain began, "he should have tried to do something."

Now the lawyer had him, "Ah, but Captain, would that not have been a complete disobedience of your order to sit and do nothing! So, based upon your own testimony, the Gunnery Sergeant did an outstanding job at following your order and should be graded such on this fitness report. Correct?"

The Gunnery Sergeant returned to full duty with a fitness report that reflected his outstanding performance of duties. It happened because the Captain did not understand the consequences of issuing instructions that if followed to the letter, gave the Gunnery Sergeant the complete right to get paid to do nothing every day.

So, when supervising an individual or a team, **ensure assigned tasks are understood, supervised, and accomplished with a successful outcome as the end result**. Here are some tips to ensure your people understand what you need them to do and how they can come to the end of a task or project with positive results.

- Once a task is assigned to an employee or a team and before you provide them with detailed instructions on how you want the work accomplished, ensure that the need for detailed instruction exists. Nothing will take away motivation from your team more than behavior that tells them you do not trust them to make the right decisions to get the task accomplished in a successful manner. Give them the task and the clearly defined goal for a successful end and let them come up with the steps to accomplish the task. Then ask them to tell you how they plan to accomplish the goal. This will allow you to provide constructive feedback and not direct their effort to the point of stifling their creative thinking.

- Ensuring your instructions are clearly understood is important so practice outlining instruction. Write them down and then ask the basic reporter question—does this instruction clearly answer the 'who, what, where, when, and how' that I wish to convey to the listener?

- Encourage your employees to ask questions about your instructions when they do not understand. Even when you make every effort to give clear and concise instructions, your listener may not fully understand what you want. Open dialog is important. Let them ask any question they feel will help them get a complete picture of your need. One way to ensure your team knows to ask questions is a simple lead in that tells them you appreciate the questions such as, "Thanks for asking that…" or "That's a good question…"

- On the other side of the coin, you should also feel free to ask your employees questions so that you can ascertain their complete understanding of your instructions. Again, a non-threating lead in can be helpful such as, "Let me be sure I was clear with my instructions…" or "So that I know I gave you good information…"

- Make sure your employees have the resources they need to accomplish the mission. If you know in advance that specific reports, documents, tools, etc. will be required to enable your team to be successful with your request, make sure they know where these can be found or provide them right up front so that the team knows you expect them to be looking at these items.

- Finally, exercise care and thought in the supervision of your team. Remember, over supervision hurts initiative and creates resentment, but under supervision will not get the job done. Is it like walking a tight rope? Absolutely, but it still comes down to the most important goal—you want your team to be successful so that they grow in confidence, so you need to ensure you help them be successful. Your leadership can make them shine when properly directed.

I worked as a database engineer for a software company that was awarded a contract with Union Pacific Railroad to write the year 2000 (Y2K) compliant software for the real estate division. One of the big milestones that we had to meet was providing the initial version of the user's manual to the real estate department so that they could begin the process of evaluating the end-product and conducting training so that, when we implemented, there would be a smooth transition from the old system to the new system. The project manager for the railroad told me up front that he thought our timeline was too aggressive and that we would never be able to deliver this first big milestone on time. He stated that the Union Pacific Information Technology (IT) Department was already complaining that they should have been allowed to address the Y2K problem internally because when the year 2000 rolled around, the real estate division would be unable to function because of our failure to provide the new software on time. He wanted me to understand just how important this one event was to set the tone for a successful project completion.

As I looked at my calendar, I knew there was no way I could meet this milestone without help. As I prepared to begin writing the detailed instructions that would be the heart of the manual, I sat down with representatives of our customer service division, sales division, IT division, and administrative support division to outline the areas where I would need their help. I was careful to define each of the related tasks, the order in which each had to be completed, how the tasks related to each other, and why this was important for the image of our company. Soon, I had people making suggestions on what tasks they could take on and how they could complete them in a timely manner. The meeting took a little over an hour, but in the end, we had a plan that allowed each division to provide support to the project and they were excited about what we could accomplish by working together.

The manual was delivered on time and the customer was very pleased with the end product. The project manager for the railroad was impressed that we were "the first outside vendor to meet every milestone in the project plan on time," and the Union Pacific IT Director was now an ally for our company. Most importantly, the internal team that worked on the manual gained confidence in our ability to meet any challenge because from this point on, we knew that if we communicated the need in clear and concise terms, we could work together to formulate a plan that would lead to success.

If you want your team to really excel, **ensure assigned tasks are understood, supervised, and accomplished** with a successful outcome as the end result. The time spent getting this right will ensure you don't go wrong.

10. Train Your Employees as a Team

As a member of the Governmental Procurement Association of Georgia, I was amazed that during the economic turndown, the attendance at our training conferences dropped dramatically. Government agencies were quickly eliminating all training dollars from their budgets and the associated travel expenses that go with off-site training in order to reduce budgets. Of course, the same agencies also instituted personnel reductions through hiring freezes or reductions in force personnel cuts and then demanded that the remaining employees "work smarter" to get the job done. Now I am not a genius, but, if you want your people to utilize the latest innovations and technology to enable them to be more effective at their assignments so that the services to the citizens and/or customers are not adversely affected (the real definition of "work smarter"), shouldn't you ensure they receive more training to enable them to succeed in reaching this goal and not less training?

If you want to create a winning team that can rise to meet the challenges we face every day in our work environments, then you need to ensure your people **receive the training they need to effectively function** at their assigned duties and, even more importantly, you need to **train together as a team.** Let's look at what you can do to maximize your training time and efforts so that it pays the biggest return on investment.

- You cannot over train your team. Every question should be seen as an opportunity to provide training to the individual and to the team, if appropriate. New challenges should be seen as a training opportunity. New projects will require new ideas and a time to train. In other words, look for an opportunity to train with your team every day. But let me caution you, do not just provide your people with the answer. It is more important you teach them how to find answers for themselves. You will get the idea when you read the closing story.

- Strive to maintain stability. We have all seen the picture of Richard Branson and the remarks that say train your people well enough so that they can leave your organization, treat them well enough that they don't leave. This simple truth will pay big dividends and strengthen your organization beyond measure.

- Encourage your team to willingly help one another. Set the example by always being available to answer questions or to help a team member with a difficult assignment. Let your team see that this is an important part of your leadership. Believe me when I tell you that they will emulate this behavior because they will see it as a positive influence to the success of the team.

- Encourage informal celebrations. Celebrate birthdays with cake and ice cream. Have a pot luck luncheon for a holiday. Celebrate the successful completion of a large project with pizza. These events build strong teams who are successful because the people care for each other and want to see every member of the team succeed. These informal celebrations are the foundation for team building.

- Never publicly blame an individual for the team's failure nor praise one individual for the team's success. Remember that you are a team and each success or failure reflects on the team as a whole. Therefore, the after-action meetings that discuss what went well and what needs attention should never be finger pointing sessions. Discuss topics, not people.

- Provide the best available facilities for your training and make maximum use of teamwork. Physically demanding occupations such as fire fighters, police special units, emergency management personnel constantly train together to ensure they are ready for any contingency they might face. The old saying, practice makes perfect, is true. So, even if you work in an office setting, you should look for innovative ways to conduct drills with your team that are relevant and will help foster a spirit of teamwork among all the members of your team.

- Ensure the training is meaningful and covers realistic topics. Nothing can cause your team to dread training time more than to have it filled with information that is not relevant to what they do every day. Since I work in the field of procurement, attending training on building codes would be interesting but would never be something I could utilize to improve my job performance. Schedule training and then ensure it is a value to your team. And do not forget to have your team members conduct most of the training sessions. The research they have to do to prepare for a presentation will cause them to grow.

- Acquaint each employee with the capabilities and limitations of all other departments so they can build mutual trust and understanding when projects cross departmental lines. If you know which department has a specific responsibility, then when that becomes necessary to a project, your team will automatically reach out and include the necessary department in the discussion and planning. You will guarantee success in this manner.

- Insist that every employee understands the functions of the other members of the team and how the team functions as part of the organization. Again, understanding the organizational structure and responsibilities will be a benefit when preparing the list of people who need to be part of the initial planning of any large project.

- Seek opportunities to train with other departments. If you want your team to understand the big picture, then they need to see how all the pieces fit together.

Let me end with an example of "tough love" training I experienced as a young sergeant in the Marine Corps. It was the early days of computers when keypunch cards were used as a data source. Other units on our base were starting to realize that simple things like pay rosters could be updated quickly by simply removing or adding a card and having a new listing run. One day, the lieutenant I worked for called me to his office. He had a list of units that wanted access to our keypunch machines so they could make full use of this new tool. Since our supply department operated 24 hours a day, 7 days a week, we could allow them access to the keypunch machines at any time. His only guidance for the scheduling was to take care of supply functions first but to be kind to the disbursing Marines since they paid us.

I sat down and analyzed the list he had provided. It was not long before I had a workable schedule hand-written on the back of a keypunch card. I returned to the lieutenant confident that he would be pleased with my results. When he asked to see the schedule, I handed him the keypunch card. He smiled and said, "Well this is wonderful. So, I can just get a handful of keypunch cards, give them to our administrative clerks on which to copy your schedule, and hand it out to the commanding officers. Why, they will be blown away with my professionalism, won't they, sergeant?"

The sarcasm lets me know I had not impressed him. "Lieutenant, I am not sure what you want?"

"A letter; a professional letter that outlines how we will meet their needs. Got it?" replied the lieutenant.

So, back at my desk, I thought about how to draft the letter.

Then I remembered that when I was sick and had to stay out of school, my mother would write a letter that explained why I should be excused. And so, I sat down and began to type, "To whom it may concern."

When I handed the letter to the lieutenant, his reaction was immediate. "To whom it may concern — I like that. So, if I don't care, I can just take this letter and…" With that, he wadded it up and threw it away. I knew I was in trouble.

"Lieutenant, I mean no disrespect but I am still not sure what you want," I stammered.

"A proper Naval letter that outlines exactly what we will do," he said quite firmly.

"Sir, I do not know how to write a Naval letter."

The lieutenant smiled, "Well, now, that I can help you with. If you will go across the hall to the administrative office, you can ask them for the Naval Correspondence Manual. This wonderful book will show you exactly what you need to do — so read it cover to cover."

I swallowed hard and retrieved the manual. I learned about cover letters, enclosures, standard subject identification codes, signing authority — so many wonderful things. I sat down and typed up the letter and the enclosure containing the schedule. I proudly returned to the lieutenant with new found confidence that he would be pleased. He reviewed the letter, handed it back, and without looking up, said, "You have a word misspelled."

Sometimes, we never learn. I replied, "Really, which one?"

Finally looking up, he said without a smile, "Look them all up and you will know."

I know this sounds like a harsh example of training. But from it, I learned that when accepting a task, I should ask enough questions so that I know exactly what will be considered a successful completion of the requirement. I learned that I may have to educate myself on new subjects to ensure the end-product meets the needs of the requester. I learned that the end-product will reflect on my professionalism so that I would always want to check and double check to ensure it was correct in every way. And I learned (and this was the point the lieutenant was trying to make as he told me later) that I would learn a lot more from the training experience if I was not just told the correct answer but had to actually train myself to find the correct answer.

Be the kind of leader that others want to follow by **training your team to be successful**.

11.Employ Your Team According to Their Capabilities

I have two brothers who are gifted athletes. I, on the other hand, got on base one time while playing little league baseball and that was because I was walked. But I wanted to be like them so badly and kept trying out for sports. The results were a definite blow to my ego as I would be cut from the team (back in the day) or I would ride the bench the whole time. I remember what brought this cycle of defeat to an end. I tried out for basketball and when the roster of who could come back for the second round of cuts was posted outside of the gymnasium, my name was not on the list. I had been cut...again. I was brokenhearted and decided to take the matter into my own hands. So, I complained about the unfairness of being cut to my mom. Surely, she would make it right. And she did—but not in the way I expected. Here was her advice.

"Len, you will never be as good at sports as your two brothers. You were not blessed with the gift of being a natural athlete like they have been. However, you have been blessed with some very wonderful gifts that they do not have. You have two choices. If you want to make the basketball team next year, you need to go to the school yard and shoot hoops, play pickup games like your brothers, use every chance you have to work on improving your ability to play. It will take a lot of work on your part but you can do it. Or, you can realize you will never be as good an athlete as your brothers and begin discovering the gifts God has given you and focus on developing those gifts. If you do that, you will be a lot happier."

Tough love? Yes. The right answer? Yes. I took her advice, focused on my strengths, and I became a much happier teenager.

You and your team will have definite strengths that enable you to be successful at many tasks. But there may be tasks that you know are outside of your team's proven abilities and because of this, you should decline to take on these tasks because you should never lead your team to failure. Therefore, it is important that you **employ your team in accordance with its capabilities**. Here are some points to consider.

- Do not volunteer your team for tasks it is not capable of completing. Not only will the team fail, which will have a devastating effect on morale, but your employees will think you are seeking personal glory at their expense.

- Keep yourself informed as to the priorities within your organization. Your team is depending on you to ensure they know how to set up their daily work schedules and to do lists. They want to make you look good by completing tasks in a timely manner but they need your help in keeping the priorities in order. So, do not let them down.

- Be sure that assignments are reasonable. If you need extra time for your team to gather necessary information and formulate a new report that your bosses have requested, ensure your bosses understand the complexities of the new report and set a reasonable expectation for providing the information. Once you have "won this battle", ensure the requirement is delivered on time and make sure it provides everything the bosses have requested. The message to your superiors will be that you are able to accommodate their demands professionally when given adequate time to accomplish the task.

- However, do not hesitate to demand the most of your employees in an emergency. There are always those emergency requirements that will take your team and you to the very edge of your capabilities and will demand extra time and effort to accomplish. By ensuring this is not the norm but is an emergency worthy of the exception, your team should be expected to support the effort and they will support the effort.

- Analyze all assignments. Don't be afraid to ask for help from supporting departments. This is why we discussed learning what other departments do and training with another department as often as possible so that when the need arises, you will have already created a cooperative atmosphere that will enable to you bring the departments together for success. And remember, once the project is done, ensure your team and all the supporting departments are recognized for their efforts.

- Assign tasks equally among your employees. Every member of your team should have the desire to prove their abilities to you. So, ensure opportunities exist for all members to lead a project, to support a project with another department, to create a training session for the team, to prepare a special report or brief, to shine. Each success will build their confidence and create a firm foundation for your team. Each struggle will be an opportunity to mentor them in specific areas and help them grow. Each assigned task will help you get to know your people, their capabilities, and their level of growth.

- Use the full capabilities of your team before requesting assistance. Yes, you will have some very hard assignments and sometimes you and your team may feel overwhelmed. But before you throw in the towel, get your team together, discuss the obstacles you are facing, and as a team, see if you can find solutions. You may be surprised at the innovation that comes from the group effort. But if you see that additional assistance will be necessary, you will know exactly what kind of assistance to ask for because the team meeting will have highlighted the deficiency without anyone on your team feeling they have failed you.

In the Marine Corps, we used to have a saying that went something like this. "I have done the difficult for so long with very little, that I can do the impossible with nothing at all in no time flat." It is a ridiculous statement. However, it was a way of life that enabled us to face even the most dangerous situations with a belief in victory. But, be assured, when I took my Marines into perilous situations, I knew they were ready, willing, and equipped to succeed because I knew where I had to be—out in front leading them.

Know what you and your team do well, know what challenges they can face and win, and **employ your team in accordance with its capabilities**. In doing so, you will create opportunities for success and enhance their willingness to stretch themselves to meet each challenge with an attitude of confidence and a winning spirit.

Part 2: Leadership Traits

12. Justice

As the Operations Director for a small county government, I worked closely with our Human Resource (HR) Department on matters of hiring, counseling, and dismissing employees. As you can imagine, the hiring part was very enjoyable. Counseling can be difficult but I was really good at outlining problems in such a way that the focus was on the success of correcting the problem and not on demeaning the employee. The results were always positive because of this approach and marginal employees quickly became loyal assets. I only had to let go of one employee and he was caught stealing money from the county so the offense and punishment were clearly outlined in the employee manual. But he was not the only employee I was told to dismiss.

A report had come in that one of our custodians was using a county vehicle to operate a trash collection business in the neighboring county and that he was conducting this business during normal business hours when he was supposed to be working in our county. The person making the report had seen him that very day operating the business. I was told that the report came from a good friend of one of our elected officials and was very credible. So, I was to dismiss the custodian that day. When I tried to say that we needed to hear the other side of the story, I was cut off and told, "I said fire him today!"

I arranged to meet with the HR Director and the custodian at the end of the work day. I began by asking him if he was in that area of the neighboring city at the time of the reported incident. He told me he was and apologized for not telling me. He went on to explain.

"Mr. Len, my ex-wife called to say that our youngest child was sick and was running a really high fever. She needed to take him to the doctor immediately. Since she had just moved into the neighborhood, she did not know anyone who could stay with our other children while she went to the doctor. So, she asked if I could come over long enough to watch the other children until she returned. I knew it was during the work hours and I should have let you know but I just felt it was important that I get there as quickly as possible because of my son's high fever. I was only there a couple of hours and I planned on working through my lunch hours until I made up the time."

"Tell me what you did when you left to come back to work and please try to include everything you did. Believe me, this is important," I said.

With a look of bewilderment on his face, he continued, "Well, my wife updated me on what the doctor said, I said bye to the kids, and I left out the back door. Oh yeah, I noticed she had a bag of trash on the back porch so I grabbed it and threw it in the back of my truck to get rid of it for her."

"And, you were in your county truck?" He nodded that he was.

So, I am faced with a dilemma. I have been told in no uncertain terms to fire this individual but I was asking myself, would that be justice?

Justice is defined as the practice of being fair and consistent. To enact justice, you must give consideration to each side of a situation and base rewards or punishment on merit.

- **Be honest with yourself about why you are making a decision.** Carefully weigh the evidence you are considering, the gravity of the infraction, the facts as presented by all sides of the argument, past performance history, and any other professional or job-related factors. Justice can only be achieved when your final decision can be defended in light of all the evidence. So, never allow your personal feeling to cloud your decision.

- **Avoid favoritism.** I usually encountered this when an employee would complain that they were counseled or written up for being late but another employee was consistently arriving late and nothing was ever said. Proving this was really easy and in most cases, the employee was correct. So, if you are leading, you must enforce all rules equally.

- **Try to be fair at all times.** If there is any doubt in your mind as to the veracity of a complaint, error on the side of justice and do what is right. This means you will have to learn to listen to the "gut" feeling that says that a story, a complaint, an accusation, is not following a logical pattern to the conclusion (or, as we used to say, does not pass the sniff test).

- **Treat all things and people in an equal manner.** This goes
  along with what I said when discussing the fact that you must
  avoid favoritism. To be an exceptional leader, you must enforce all the rules in the same manner in every circumstance
  and with every person.

So, have you thought about what you would do to ensure
justice in the opening story? Let me outline the actions I took
that I felt handled this situation in the most appropriate manner.

A little more probing revealed that the person who made the
accusation lived next door to his ex-wife and he was constantly
complaining that the children were too loud when they played
outside. It made it hard for him to watch his television. My employee and the neighbor had exchanged angry words concerning
him yelling at the children just a few days earlier. Therefore, it became clear that the complaint was not true and was made for the
sole purpose of damaging my employee's professional standing
with the county. So, here was what I did.

I made it very clear to him that he had an absolute obligation
to let us know when he had to take off in the middle of the day
for a personal matter and that his failure to do this had placed
himself in jeopardy of losing his job because of the neighbor's
false accusation. I emphasized that I was not upset that he needed
time to take care of his children; I truly respected him for that.
However, I stressed that he demonstrated poor judgment in that
he did not advise anyone of the emergency and that it was because of the lack of judgment he had displayed that I would have
to take corrective action. I then let him know that I was suspend-

ing him for one day without pay to give him time to consider the gravity of the matter and to reflect on what his action should be if this happens again in the future.

When the custodian left, he thanked me for being fair and not firing him. Of course, once he left my office, the Human Resource Director reminded me that I was now in trouble because I was ordered to fire him. I asked her a very simple question. "Would you have fired him once you uncovered all the facts?"

The person who ordered me to fire him was furious with me and demanded I call the custodian back in and fire him. I let him know we did not have grounds to fire him and that my handling of the situation would stand up to any court in the land. He begrudgingly relented when he saw the HR Director nod her head in agreement.

Do you want to be an exceptional leader? Then be guided by justice when dealing with your people.

13. Judgment

In the early 1990s, a directive came out of Headquarters, Marine Corps stating the single male and female Marines who lived in the barracks should be allowed to visit each other in their rooms since this was their "home." Commands were required to write an order that allowed for this practice but would ensure that the highest values of respect and moral character were maintained. I was the Executive Officer (XO) of an enlisted Marine training command at the time where we had five different courses of instruction. After discussion with the Commanding Officer (CO), an updated Barracks Order was written which allowed male and females Marines to visit each other's rooms until 10:00 pm, the official time of "lights out." At 9:55 pm, the Fire Watches were to knock on all the doors to the rooms and announce a five-minute warning to ensure "mistakes" were prevented. Sounds simple, right? But alas, the hearts of young Marines can throw a wrench into the most well thought out plans.

One night, at 10:05, a female Lance Corporal (LCpl) came to the Sergeant on duty in the barracks and told him that she was walking outside and through the windows, she noticed that a female Private First Class (PFC) had a male Marine in her room after lights out. The Sergeant went and knocked on the door to the room and two very sleepy Marines came to the door. The Sergeant advised them that they had violated the barracks order concerning visitations and took them to the duty office to fill out the report of the violation. He then ordered them to return to their individual rooms and to report to him in the morning. He marched them to the First Sergeant's office in the morning and provided a report of the incident.

Upon investigating, it was discovered that the female LCpl and the female PFC both liked the same male PFC. He liked the female PFC much to the dismay of the LCpl. That night, while the two PFC's were studying in the female PFC's room for a test, they fell asleep—one at the desk and one in a chair. The LCpl happened to be walking by the room and saw that they were asleep at 9:50 pm. She quickly went to the female Marine wing of the barracks and told the Fire Watch not to announce the five-minute warning because she was there and she would do it for him. He took her at her word and went off to announce the warning in the other wings of the barracks. The LCpl never made the announcement and then reported them to the Sergeant on duty.

So, we have two Marines who absolutely violated our barracks order but they were set up! However, if they were to get away with the "we fell asleep" defense, it would soon become the defense for all the other Marines so they could get away with the same offense. How would you punish these Marines in a manner that would send a message to all the other Marines that there are no excuses for violating orders but the punishment would also be fair considering all the circumstances surrounding the violation?

While you think about how you would have handled this situation, let's pause and consider how important good judgment is in situations like this. Judgment is your ability to think about things clearly, calmly, and in an orderly fashion so that you can make good decisions. To enable you to act and make a fair judgment, let me share the things that should be considered when you have a difficult situation to handle that involves the personal feelings of your employees so that you can ensure you are fair to all parties concerned but also ensures the "drama" ends and work resumes.

- **Know what the policies say**. Since I was privy to the policy discussion and had helped review the rewritten barracks order, I knew the history of the order, the logic behind the content of the order, and the conduct that needed to happen that would constitute a violation of the order. This would be absolutely important to the final outcome and is a must for any leader.

- **Thoroughly investigate**. If you have more than one child, you know that when they get into an argument, there is "his" story, "her" story, and somewhere in between, the truth. Treat every investigation in the same manner. Ask questions and seek answers based on your knowledge of the policies. Don't stop until you are thoroughly satisfied you can logically answer the questions as to who, what, where, when, and how. You have to be assured in the end that those who are responsible are held accountable for any infraction but that you were also fair in your judgment.

- **Know your options**. Once you have determined that an infraction of policies has been committed, that those responsible knew they were violating established policies, and that corrective action must be taken, you need to know what you may do to correct the problem without overstepping your authority.

- **Ensure the punishment also provides a lesson learned**. When we punish our children, we try to ensure they learn a lesson from their mistake. So, when we put them in time out, we will ask them to tell us why they ended up there and what they should have done to not be punished. Approach difficult and sensitive errors in judgment the same way.

So, what would you have done with the above real life situation? Our CO was so unsure of what he needed to do that he scheduled a Friday off and told me to handle this situation before he returned the following Monday. I spoke with the First Sergeant and Administrative Officer to get their input and they let me know that they were stumped as to what should be done to ensure there would be no breakdown in the good order and discipline of our Command. I felt absolutely alone but I knew I had to get this right. Here is what I did.

Punishment for minor offenses in the Marine Corps is accomplished at legal proceedings called "Office Hours." As a Captain, I had the authority to reduce these Marines by one rank and fine them two-thirds of their pay for up to two months and restrict them to the barracks for up to 30 days. I could even sentence them to the brig for up to ten days. I could combine these punishments in any manner I saw fit and could vary the length of any fine or restriction. I could also impose punishment and then suspend all or a portion of the punishment for up to six months if I so desired so that the Marine had to "toe the line" for a while. In other words, these Marines were facing serious consequences for their "naps."

I had the First Sergeant schedule the Office Hours for that Friday. I told him I wanted the following groups assembled. The two Marines being charged. The LCpl who reported the incident and the Marine who was the Fire Watch at the time of the incident would be gathered as official witnesses. Told him the Office Hours would be held in the conference room and that I wanted the five Senior Marines in charge of each of our courses there, the Sergeant who was on duty that night, and I wanted one Marine from every class we had in session and one Marine from the barracks detail who was waiting to "class up" to be in the conference room as official observers to the Office Hours.

At exactly 2:00 pm, I marched into the conference room where about 20 Marines had been assembled and took my place behind a podium. They snapped to attention. I gave the command, "At Ease" and I told the First Sergeant to call the Marines being charged. They reported in front of the podium and stood at attention as I began reading the charges against them and reading the approved script that ensures that all legal requirements are followed during the proceedings. When I got to the part where I ask those charged were there any mitigating circumstances that caused them to disobey the visitation orders, they stated that they had fallen asleep.

I looked bewildered. "First Sergeant, isn't the Fire Watch supposed to knock on doors and announce a five-minute warning? It appears this did not happen. Get the Marine who was walking Fire Watch in here now."

The Fire Watch explained that he had been instructed not to provide the announcement in the woman Marines wing because the LCpl stated she would do it for him. "First Sergeant, get the LCpl in here."

I had already officially counseled the LCpl for her part in this situation and she was now about to face her punishment. She had to stand before the assembly and admit that she had set up the two Marines to get in trouble and that she did so with malicious intent. The looks they gave her were far worse than any punishment I could have handed down to her. She knew that she had lost the trust of these Marines. From this point until her graduation, she would not be seen as a leader among her fellow Marines.

I announced I was suspending the proceedings and asked the two Marines facing charges to step outside. "I have a real problem with what I have heard. Basically, this is equivalent to giving these two Marines brand new rifles and sending them out to defeat an enemy position without giving them any ammunition. They were set up to die. My job is to maintain the good order and discipline of this unit by ensuring that those who violate orders are properly punished. But how can I ensure the message is sent to all my Marines that all my barracks regulations must be followed without exception. If I do not administer punishment for their violation of my orders then the order becomes worthless — good order and discipline then go out the window. But the system put in place to ensure this kind of excuse would not be acceptable failed due to malicious intent. What am I as the leader to do?"

Now the fun began. I walked in front of each of the Marines in the room and looked them in the eye and asked, "What am I to do as the leader to ensure my Marines understand the importance of following all legal orders without question while still dispensing justice in this case?" As you can guess, no one had an answer for me. I was about to give them the answer.

I had the two Marines report back to me and I pronounced my judgment. "I am suspending these proceedings in total. You will not be receiving any formal punishment for violating my barracks orders. (A look of instance relief spread across their faces.) However, that does not mean you will not be punished. (Now another surprised look and the faces of the observers were glued to me.) This weekend, each of you will write me a 1,000-word essay on the importance of observing my barracks regulations. The essays will be presented to me in my office by 8 o'clock Monday morning. These essays will be typed — no signs of corrections on any page and not one misspelled word. Your instructor will ensure you have access to a typewriter, plenty of paper, and a dictionary for your weekend assignment. These essays must be good. After I read them and approve them, they will be placed on the "Must Read" bulletin board in the barracks that contains all the instructions and information newly arriving Marines to our Command must read. You will be ensuring that future Marines know that there will be no tolerance for disobeying my orders whether I am still here or have moved on in my career. Do you understand? (A quick "Yes, Sir")

Then I looked at the gallery, "So, Marines, when you go back to your rooms, what will you tell your fellow Marines? Will you let them know that these two Marines got away with violating my orders or will you tell them that today, you saw that you can trust your Marine leaders to administer justice in a way that punishment is not punishing? I hope you learned the right lesson today." As I turned to walk from the room, the First Sergeant gave the expected "Attention on deck" and my Marines snapped to attention.

I knew before I even entered the room exactly what I was going to do and how I was going to draw the observers in so that they would understand the gravity of being a leader. I wanted them to understand that leadership is about caring for your people in a manner that they learn from mistakes and grow in the process while ensuring the good order and discipline of the unit. The essays that were written were really good and were properly placed on the "Must Read" bulletin board. The Command experienced a surge in pride as every Marine learned the facts surrounding the final judgment and gained a better understanding of the difficult decisions that face those in a position of leadership.

If you are going to be an exceptional leader, you must be willing to face difficult situations and decisions with a thorough understanding of all the facts and then provide a solution that demonstrates fairness, justice, and compassion. You are going to need to develop exceptional judgment.

14. Dependability

The Supply Officer had called the Warehouse Officer and me into his office. "Gentlemen, I have decided to have you two swap positions. Lieutenant, you have a lot of potential so you need to become more familiar with how the computerized system works so going to the Stock Control Section to manage the computer input and output will be a good learning experience. Len will be able to help you transition and grow since he will be right next door in your old office. Go ahead and get your stuff together to make the move today. I need to talk to Len about the warehouse."

The Major paused as the Lieutenant thanked him for the opportunity and left the office. Once the Lieutenant closed the door, I received my instructions. "Len, the Master Sergeant (affectionately known as 'Top' in the Marine Corps) in the warehouse is on the ROAD (Retired On Active Duty—means he shows up each day but does nothing to contribute to the accomplishment of the mission). He either needs to make it official and retire or he needs to get back to work. That is why you are going to the warehouse. It is your responsibility to make one or the other happen but I am not going to tolerate his lack of motivation any longer. Do you have any questions?" A quick "No, Sir" and I was dismissed to begin this challenge.

The Major was upset because the Master Sergeant was no longer dependable. Dependability means that you can be relied upon to perform your duties properly. It means you can be trusted to complete a job. It is the willing and voluntary support of policies. It means putting your best effort forth to attempt to achieve the highest standards of performance. In the Corps, if you are not dependable in garrison, then I know that I cannot count on you should we go to war. That is where the Top stood and I had to change his attitude quickly.

By lunchtime, the Lieutenant and I had successfully moved to our new offices and brought our teams together to announce the changes being made. Right after lunch, I invited the Top to join me in my office (which was located such that you had to walk through the Top's office to get to mine — something I would be able to use to my advantage).

Before I tell you how I approached my problem, let me tell you the things that I took into consideration as I decided what I needed to do to bring the Top back on board.

- **Know what motivates the person you are trying to re-energize**. In the case of the Top, I knew that he took great pleasure in chewing people out for mistakes. I would use this to my advantage until I retrained him to approach corrective action in a better manner.

- **Know the behavior you want to correct and target your action accordingly**. In this case, the Top just did not seem to care anymore. He came to work late each morning, left early for lunch but returned late, and left early each day. Once at work, he sat in his office and if he needed to talk to someone, they had to come to his office. I needed to get him out of his office so he could see the problems.

- **Know how you are going to demonstrate the behavior you want so they have a positive example to follow**. If I was going to get the Top back on board, he had to know that I was committed to the overall success of the team. I had to have a plan that kept both of us motivated.

- **Know exactly how to correct them when they fail**. In all likelihood, the Top would resist at first and might even push back. When this happens, I had to be ready to correct him in a professional manner that re-enforced the desired outcome. That way, correction is positive but swift.

So, now let me share my solution with you. As the Top settled into the chair in front of my desk, I began to outline my plan. "So, Top, let me tell you how I will start each day. I will come in at about 7:30 am each morning, get a cup of coffee, a clipboard with a tablet, and a pen. I am going to walk around the warehouse and write down things I find that need to be corrected before the end of the day. I expect you to do the same thing. At eight o'clock, you and I will meet in my office to compare our lists. If you find something that I did not note or you find the same thing that I found, you may call anyone into your office and do whatever is necessary to get the problem fixed by the end of the day. However, if I find something that you do not find, you have to get someone to fix it but you MUST ask them to do so nicely—no yelling, no hollering, no threatening. Then, at 4:00 pm each day, you and I will walk the warehouse together to ensure that everything has been corrected to my satisfaction. Any questions?"

"No, Sir," he said with a smile.

The next morning, I was sitting in the Top's office when he arrived for work at 8:15 am. "Good morning, Top," I said, "we are a little late getting our first meeting started. Get your list and let's start comparing."

"Sir, I have not made my list yet. Let me get settled and we can meet in a little while."

I had expected this was going to happen. "Well, then, Top, your list is empty. Get a tablet and get ready to write while I outline what I found." The Top sat at his desk and began to take notes on what I had found and what I wanted done to correct each problem. Once I was done, I went to my office to see what happened next. I heard the Top give a list of names to one of the Marines walking by and that he wanted them in his office now. My fun was about to begin.

Once the Marines were gathered in the Top's office, he began to rant and rave about being embarrassed. I quickly joined them in the office, "Top, please ask these Marines to step outside for a moment. An emergency has just come up and we need to talk." The Marines filed outside and closed the door behind them.

I smiled at the Top and began to shake my finger at him as I said in a very polite tone, "No way, Top. Remember our rule.

You did not find anything this morning so you can't yell at these Marines. You have to ask them nicely to please fix the problems by the end of the day. So, now, you are going to call them back in here, apologize for raising your voice, and ask them nicely to PLEASE fix these problems and that you and I will be checking on them at the end of the day. And remember, I am right here so I will hear every word you speak." Now the smile faded and with steely eyes, I punctuated my request, "Got it!"

The next morning, when I arrived at 7:30 am, the Top was there waiting with his list. "I am ready for our meeting, Sir."

"Good, Top, I will meet you at 8:00 am like I told you in the beginning," as I walked to my office trying to hide the smile on my face. Not only was the Top back on board, but over time, I was able to change the way he interacted with our Marines so that we became a dynamic team.

If you are going to be an exceptional leader, you must learn how to motivate all your people so that they want to give their all every day.

15. Initiative

For Marines and sailors, shipboard deployments mean separation from your family for six months and that separation gets even harder when you are deployed during the Christmas holiday. Being faced with this situation, I remembered the example of some fine officers from my days as an enlisted Marine and I came up with an idea. Why not have the officers of our squadron serve the Christmas meal to the enlisted Marines and sailors?

As a Marine Aviation Supply Officer, I was "dual hatted" on deployments which meant I worked for the Marine helicopter squadron and the ship's supply officer. Being in this unique position would make getting this plan set up easier for me than for other officers. So, my first discussion was with the ship's supply officer who had control over all "mess" decks (military for dining facility). I asked him that if our Commanding Officer (CO) agreed to my plan, would he allow the Marine officers of our squadron to serve the Christmas meal on the enlisted mess deck. He thought that this was a wonderful suggestion and agreed to work with the squadron to allow our officers to man one of the serving lines. I told him I would get back to him quickly.

My next visit was to the squadron CO. I outlined my suggestion to him and he was on board quickly. He told me to put a sign-up sheet in ready room (where the pilots gather to do their flight briefs and hang out between flights). I was to put his name at the top of the list, the executive office's (XO) name next, and then my name. Once we knew how many officers would be willing to participate, the CO told me to get with him and we would lay out the final arrangements.

Much to my delight, every single officer from our squadron signed up to serve. So, with the help of the CO and XO, a rotating schedule was set up showing what times everyone would have to be on the mess deck to serve the Christmas meal. The CO even loosened the uniform standards indicating that "red noses, antlers, Santa Claus hats, garland, and Christmas decorations added to the uniform would be considered as appropriate dress for the occasion."

Coordinating with the ship's supply officer and his enlisted mess deck officer, we had everything ready on Christmas Day. Much to the surprise and delight of our Marines and sailors, they were greeted with a Merry Christmas and what would you like on your plate from some very odd looking Santa Clauses, reindeer, and Christmas trees. Frowns turned to smiles and there was a lot of laughter coming from our serving line.

As a leader, your willingness to take the initiative is vital to your leadership character. Here is what I mean by taking initiative.

- **Initiative is seeing what needs to be done and taking action even though no one has told you to do something about**

the situation. Your action may not be something even seen by other people but makes a difference. For example, I arrive early to work every day at my office where I work for the Jackson County Government (old Marine habits are hard to break). Walking from my car to the door that I enter, I will sometimes see trash that has been dropped or blown into the parking lot. I always take the time to pick it up and dispose of it properly. Why? Because the parking lot is the first thing our citizens see when they visit our offices and it should reflect the pride we have in our county.

- **Initiative means you will meet new and unexpected situations with prompt action**. The building in which I work is a maze of hallways and offices that are the results of additions being added on over many years. As a result, finding a particular office can sometimes be tricky. So, when someone comes to our area and is in the wrong location, I walk them to the proper office. I ask their name and purpose for their visit along the way so that when we walk into the appropriate office, I can introduce them, state their problem, and then turn them over to an employee who will be able to help them.

- **Initiative includes using resourcefulness to get something done without the normal materials or methods being available to you**. There have been times when I receive a call from a citizen with a complaint that has nothing to do with my purchasing function. I always listen and then tell them which office they should have called, the name of the county employee to whom they need to speak, and the phone number they will need in the future. I then obtain the best phone number to call them back should we get cut off and I then transfer their call. I will call them later just to ensure their complaint is being addressed. This sets an important impression that the County cares about the concerns of our citizens.

- **Initiative means staying mentally and physically alert so that you can be aware of what needs to be done and will be capable of doing it without being told.** Because we work in a building that was built in 1939, the water coming out of the old pipes is not very good for drinking. We have several water coolers throughout the building that hold five-gallon water bottles. These are heavy and can be tricky to replace. But I keep my eyes on them because many of our offices only have women in them. So, when I see an empty bottle, I obtain a full bottle from the storage area and replace it so they do not have to be concerned about this. I do this not because they are not capable of replacing the bottle themselves, but because they should not have to replace the bottle when I am available to do it for them.

Does taking the initiative pay in the long run? Absolutely; let me share the final part of the opening story.

That evening, the squadron CO attended the nightly meeting with the Captain of the ship, the ship's XO, the ship department heads, and the Marine commanding officers that were aboard the ship. The ship's Captain started the meeting by complementing our squadron CO for having his officers serve the enlisted sailors and Marines their Christmas meal. He then looked at the Navy officers and said, "My only question is, why were there no Navy officers serving our troops?" The CO told me he took full responsibility for the idea but told me when it was time for my evaluation, he would not forget what I did to make him look good.

In the Corps, we had an old saying. There are those who make things happen, there are those who watch things happen, and there are those who wonder what happened. Don't just let things happen or wonder what happened. If you want to be an exemplary leader, take the initiative and make things happen.

16. Decisiveness

I have often mentioned with much pride that I spent twenty wonderful years serving the people of this great nation as a United States Marine. I had an amazing career. I enlisted at the age of eighteen and after three months of boot camp, I earned the title of Marine at the rank of private. Before I retired, I had achieved the rank of Captain and had worked for some of the greatest leaders in the Marine Corps who helped shape me to be a better person. They willingly taught me to embrace the principles of leadership that shaped the success of the Marine Corps from the time Captain Robert Barrows walked into Tun Tavern and announced that he was looking for good men to be the very first United States Marines (yes, the Marine Corps started in a bar).

I would love to tell you that my decision to join the Marine Corps was all about my desire to serve our Country, to be a part of the very best military service in America, or to willingly lay down my life for the just causes of our leaders. But that would be a lie. I made a hasty decision that would impact my life forever—thankfully in a positive manner. But before I tell you my story, let me talk about the importance of decisiveness in a leader.

Decisiveness means that you are able to make good decisions

without delay. Being able to do this is not easy, especially when the crisis requires an immediate decision and you have the lives of others in your hands as we did in the Marine Corps. But taking the time to work on the skills that will help you gain confidence in your decision-making process will ensure that when the time comes, you will make the best possible decision in any crisis. When you are faced with a challenge, here are some things that will help you come to the right decision.

- **Get all the facts and weigh them against each other**. This is the hardest part of making a quick decision in a crisis. You may have only limited information at your disposal at the time. But, you have got to learn to weigh the known facts and couple that knowledge with your experience to come up with a solution that will begin the process of heading you and your team in the direction of success. You may have to make adjustments along the way, but you will be acting and that will inspire confidence in your team.

- **Act calmly and quickly**. No matter how big the problem, you must present yourself with calmness to your team. They may be feeling a sense of panic and have come to you because they expect you to restore their feeling that everything is going to be okay. Yes, they are looking for a solution, but the unspoken request is for leadership. Be the calm in the storm and inspire confidence in your team.

- **Announce your decision in a clear, firm, professional man-**

ner. After listening to all the known facts and adding in your experience with similar situations, clearly outline the plan of action, be positive and professional in laying out the plan, and begin assigning the necessary tasks to your team to begin those actions that will bring about the positive change they are so desperately seeking. By leading your people from crisis to action, you will inspire confidence in your team.

- **Practice being positive in your actions instead of acting half-hearted or changing your mind on an issue**. Finally, utilize the above skills for every decision you make so that when the crisis hits, you are ready to react in a positive manner. Let your team see that you are methodical in your problem analysis and can be trusted to work with the team to cultivate success. Adjusting the plan to meet a new circumstance is acceptable, but constantly changing the plan because you really do not have a firm grasp on the situation will cause your team to stop following. Be ready to lead and you will inspire confidence in your team.

So, how did I start my career in the Corps? I took all the entrance examines and the induction physical during my senior year in high school because it was an excused absence from school and a free lunch. I had no intention of joining the Corps. Right after graduation, I found out that the full-time job I had been promised at the local newspaper office where I was to begin the process of becoming a pressman in the press room was not going to materialize. That was devastating news and I did not know what to do other than to continue working there until I found a full-time job. My girlfriend at the time had graduated from another local high school and she and I had not been able to see each other for the last two weeks. The night I found out I would have to find a full-time job, we were supposed to get together. So, I went to work cleaning the presses in the late afternoon and hurried home to get ready for my date.

When I got home, I quickly got cleaned up and then helped my older brother take some of his personal items to his new apartment since he was moving out of the house and going out on his own. I returned home to grab something before heading to my girlfriend's house. To my surprise, the Marine recruiter and two of my friends were sitting in the kitchen talking to my mom. The recruiter asked me for a minute of my time and began outlining how I could go to boot camp on the buddy program with my two friends so I would have the comfort of starting my Marine Corps career with two people I knew and trusted. Thus, began a long conversation on why that was a silly idea and that I was never going to be a Marine. And by a long conversation, I mean that I lost track of time and before I knew it, it was 10:00 pm and the phone was ringing. You can guess who it was and she was not very happy. My mom handed me the phone and my girlfriend lit into me about how she had gotten ready for our date and how she had been waiting and how I must not care for her feelings and on and on and on.

Just graduated from high school, no full-time job, and a screaming girlfriend. Time to make a decision, based on the facts I had. I finally interrupted my girlfriend and said, "You will not be able to yell at me anytime you want again." I hung up the phone, looked at the recruiter, and asked him, "When did you say I would leave?"

His reply was simple—in nine days. "I'll go," I replied calmly and quickly, announcing my decision in a firm, professional manner.

Nine days later, at about midnight, I arrived at Parris Island, South Carolina—the east coast home of Marine Corps boot camp. The Sergeant at the new arrival processing center was yelling at me. He was wondering who had given my father and mother permission to have children, knowing the results would be someone as inept as me (yes, I cleaned that up). As he was yelling in my ear, all I could think was, "You need to learn to make better decisions." My leadership training had started.

If you are going to be an exceptional leader, you must be able to make the difficult decisions in a timely manner so that you inspire confidence in your team.

17. Tact

After a long day, I was always grateful when I got to my apartment and could unwind from the stress of the day. As I placed my foot on the step to walk up to my second-floor apartment, I heard the door open to the corner apartment and the elderly lady who lived there walked out. To my surprise, she began to speak to me.

"Excuse me. Have you tasted those new international coffees that they have been advertising on TV? I bought some today and have heated some water. I was wondering if you would like to join me for a cup of coffee."

I was shocked. I had lived upstairs for at least six months and had said hello to this neighbor a couple of times, but that was it. Because my mother had taught me to always respect my elders, I knew exactly what to do. "Why thank you, ma'am," I said as I walked toward her door, "it would be my pleasure. My name is Len." I extended my hand and gave her a gentle hand shake.

We looked at the different coffees and selected the flavor we thought would be best. As she began to prepare our coffee, she told me to go ahead and have a seat at the head of the table. As I prepared to sit down, I could not help but notice that two table lamps were sitting right in front of the chair in which I was about to sit. "Ma'am, do you want me to move these lamps?"

I was about to get a wonderful lesson in the art of tact.

In the Marine Corps, we jokingly defined tact as the ability to tell someone to go to hell and have them thank you for the travel advice. However, being tactful means you know how to deal with people in a manner that will ensure good relations and avoid problems. To accomplish this, always remember:

- **Be polite and courteous**. Nothing breaks down barriers faster than good manners. You will automatically send the message that you are going to treat the person you are engaging with dignity and respect. Their natural reaction will be to treat you in the same manner. The Golden Rule (treat others as you wish to be treated) really is important.

- **Remain calm**. This is especially important when you are facing a big challenge that may seem daunting to the other person or to your team. Be prepared with the facts and present your plan in a professional manner that clearly conveys the message that "we will work together to accomplish the impossible."

- **Be firm**. Being tactful does not mean you allow anyone to walk all over you. You are attempting to steer a person or your team in a direction that will guarantee success. You need not be ashamed of doing that so as politely and calmly as you can, present your position in a manner that helps them see the positive results and the rewards that come from a job well done.

So, how did my sweet neighbor teach me an important lesson in tact that night? As she brought me my coffee, she explained how the lamps reminded her of a trip she took with her husband who had passed away a couple of years earlier. She wanted to continue using them because of the wonderful memories they represented but the cords were frayed and she was afraid they were now too dangerous to use. If only she knew someone who could rewire them for her. She had purchased what she needed to rewire them but just had no idea how to fix them herself.

Why she was in luck. I had learned to rewire a lamp back in high school shop class. Because she was so kind as to share her international coffee with me, it just seemed the right thing to do so I offered to rewire the lamps for her. She was so surprised but quickly retrieved the items she had purchased from the hardware store. (Seeing a whole reel of lamp cord and a full bag of plugs should have been a warning but I just figured she did not realize she did not need all these items for two lamps). As I sipped my coffee, I began the process of rewiring the lamps while she shared the wonderful story of how she and her husband had found them and purchased them.

Once I was done, I asked her where she would like me to place the lamps. She told me she had moved one of her bedroom lamps to one of the end tables temporarily and if I would replace the lamps on the end tables and then put the other lamp back to her bedroom she would really appreciate it. As I went to un-plug the lamp that was to be returned to the bedroom, I noticed that the cord on this lamp was also in bad shape. I told her that this lamp really needed new wiring also and that I better check the other one that was in the bedroom. Before long, I was now rewriting these lamps for her while she told me the story of how her husband had surprised her with these lamps as an anniversary gift. Before the night was over, I had rewired every lamp in her apartment, the light in her china cabinet, and really began to understand what a wonderful man her husband was as she talked of their many travels and the story behind so many items in her home. And can you believe it? She had just the right amount of plugs in the bag from the hardware store to complete this task.

I knew long before I left her apartment that my neighbor had carefully set me up so that I would end up taking care of all her lamps. But the very tactful way that she was able to get me to volunteer to do the first couple of lamps so that I felt good about helping her always stuck with me. I knew if I could learn to be as tactful, I could not only lead my people, I could do so in a manner that encouraged them to follow me.

My mom always told me that you will catch more flies with honey than you will with vinegar. I now understand exactly what she was trying to teach me. If you want to be an exceptional leader, then utilize the tool called tact to encourage your team to follow you, not because you said so, but because they are able to see and share in your vision.

18. Integrity

"When it comes time to award that bid, make sure Company ABC gets the bid."

I was surprised to hear this coming from an elected official. I began to explain, "What you are asking me to do is called bid rigging and it is against the law. If I do this and we get caught, then what will happen is you will disavow any knowledge of this conversation and I will end up going to jail. Since I do not know you that well, I am not willing to go to jail for you. So, I will assume that since you are a newly elected official, you have not had your ethics class yet and therefore you were not aware that this type of request is not appropriate."

I lost my nice big office and was moved to a small office on the bottom floor of the building for taking this stand. I would like to say it stopped here but it did not.

"Here are the changes you need to make to your request for proposals because I just am not going to do the job the way you have requested."

This was a vendor who was about to present a proposal for a project. When I asked him what made him think he had the right to come in and demand changes to the proposal documents, his answer floored me.

"Elected Official XYZ has guaranteed me that I will be awarded this project so you need to get on board and get these changes out so my proposal matches your requirements."

He did not get the project. I lost some of my responsibilities and authority because the requirements were not changed and his proposal was disqualified for not meeting the specifications. However, Elected Official XYZ was able to get all the proposals tossed out and I was ordered to prepare a new request for proposals with new requirements. I received another visit from the vendor.

"You screwed me once. You will not do it again. I get this proposal or else, got it?"

He not only did not get the project but one of his associates actually stated that they were promised the job by Elected Official XYZ in a public meeting which caused a very awkward moment for the elected official. The personal attacks became unbearable. I left the job.

Integrity is defined in the Webster's New College Dictionary, copyright 1960 (yes, I love my old dictionary for writing) as "moral soundness; honesty; uprightness." It is not something we can touch, feel, or hold in our hand. It is a part of your character as a human being and you either have it or you do not. And in today's environment, it seems to be missing at every level of leadership. There are volumes of articles that outline why this has happened so I am not going to focus on what went wrong. But here are the reasons we need to re-ignite this characteristic in our business environment.

- As a leader, once your people know that you are willing to bend the rules and look the other way, they will never trust you again. No matter how you try to justify it to them, they will know that you put yourself and your advancement above everything else. They will always be leery of your motives from that day forward. And once you have lost their trust, you have lost your team.

- Understand what you will lose. In the above examples, I knew that if I had given in the very first time I was asked to compromise my integrity, I would have to do it every time I was asked. I would be a "slave" to whims of a corrupt system. Never give anyone this kind of control over yourself. Be polite, be professional, but say no to any behavior that compromises your integrity.

- Understand that you will become a constant reminder of the bad behavior. Just as you become the puppet once you compromise your behavior and must now dance at the beck and call of your bosses, you will also be someone they cannot trust to protect them should the inappropriate actions come to light. So, instead of being a valued team member, you will have become a constant threat and they will find a way to eventually get you out of the organization. And don't be surprised if they use your lack of integrity as the very means to destroy you.

- Understand that there is a cost to standing firm and maintaining your integrity. I eventually left a job that I enjoyed and a job where I was adding value to our citizens by building a very efficient and effective government operation. Had I not left, I am sure the retaliation I experienced for staying true to my principles would have gotten worse. I knew the cost before I said no the first time and was willing to pay that price. So, you may end up with your integrity intact but still be looking for a new job. Trust me, it is worth it.

I had a friend who was feeling pressure in his job to compromise his integrity to make his bosses happy. I could see he was really having a hard time dealing with the pressure. So, I shared in more detail the examples I shared at the beginning of this article. I then told him that after I left my job, each morning, I would get up and have to look into the mirror to wash my face, shave, and brush my teeth. And each morning, I liked the person who was looking back at me. I reminded him that had I compromised my integrity, I would have eventually lost my job anyways but the difference would be that when I looked into the mirror each morning, I would hate the person looking back at me.

His answer was so telling. "But you do not understand. I need this job. I really have a lot of debt!"

Alas, he finally did what he felt he needed to do to keep everyone happy and ended up losing the job just as I predicted — with his reputation soiled.

If you are ever going to be an exceptional leader, then integrity must be your very first leadership characteristic to guard and protect.

19. Enthusiasm

Do you get out of bed each morning ready to take on the challenges of the day? Does the idea of going to work fill you with excitement? Can you visualize the improvements you have accomplished and the changes that will continue to improve your performance and the performance of your team? If you answered yes to these questions, most people will say you are crazy. But in truth, you have discovered how enthusiasm can make the difference between going to work each day and going to another day of adventure at your chosen occupation.

Enthusiasm is defined as a sincere interest and exuberance in the performance of your duties. It is characterized by being optimistic, cheerful, and willing to accept challenges. It is a characteristic of leadership that is completely within your control. You choose to either see each day as an exciting challenge or as just another day at the office. But embracing a spirit of enthusiasm for your job will pay big benefits. They are:

- Your enthusiasm will set the tone for your team members. Whether your team members will admit it or not, when you present a project, a new system, a change in daily operating routines, or any other change that can cause them anxiety, they become apprehensive. However, when you outline all the wonderful benefits this change will bring to the team and to the organizational strategy, your team will approach the change with an attitude of "we can" instead of "not again." Enthusiasm is contagious.

- When you create an enthusiastic work environment, creativity becomes the norm. I remember working with the programmer in the Navy and Marine Corps to help create new reports and fix "bugs" for our supply computer system. Everyone really enjoyed what we were doing to create value for the combat mission of our ships and aviation units through our computer support. Some of the solutions we came up with were amazing because of the excitement that could be felt when working through the problem. Later, when the programming was turned over to civilians, the one comment I heard over and over was, "Wow, we would have never come up with that solution to the problem. That is ingenious."

- Enthusiasm can turn even an everyday, mundane task into something special — not because it is exciting — but because you were able to successfully complete a required task. Enthusiasm sees success in even the simple tasks.

So, does creating enthusiasm work? You bet it does.

As the warehouse officer for the aviation supply department in Hawaii, I stressed the importance of keeping the warehouse neat and clean for safety purposes to my Top (senior enlisted Marine). Despite everything he tried, the warehouse still was not meeting my expectations. Finally, the Top came to me to seek advice on how to get the results that I was expecting.

"Glad you asked, Top," I began, "Here is what to do. Divide the warehouse into three distinct sections using reflective tape. Go to the sign shop and get nice signs made with the names of each of the three Sergeants assigned to our warehouse. Hang one sign in each of the sections and call the three Sergeants together. Tell them this. Each of them is responsible for the cleanliness of their section. They do not have to clean the section alone because they have junior Marines who should be helping them. But they are responsible for the cleanliness of their sections and any problems will be a reflection of their leadership."

"Now," I continued, "the day after you have made the assignments, call the three together in the morning and tell one of them, and it does not matter which one, that his section really looked good. Then walk away and watch what happens."

The Top put my plan into practice and was amazed that by the end of the week, the warehouse looked great. He came to me and said, "Sir, it looks good now but how do we keep it this way?"

"Simple, Top, each Monday, gather the Sergeants together and tell one of them that his area is the best looking area — never name the same Sergeant two weeks in a row — and they will constantly strive to get your approval. The positive feedback will create the enthusiasm in them to get the job done. No yelling; no fussing; just leadership."

Being in a position of leadership is such an honor. You

have the opportunity to be a positive influence for the organization, your team, and each person with whom you lead. Thinking about this each morning should excite you to begin another day full of positive energy. Just being the leader should bring about enthusiasm. Get enthused and be an exceptional leader.

20. Bearing

I missed my 21st birthday. I was a Sergeant in the Marine Corps and was at Norton Air Force Base waiting to fly to Okinawa, Japan on the day before my birthday. We took off very late that night and by the time we landed at Kadena Air Force Base on the island of Okinawa, it was the day after my birthday.

But I was not worried about missing this important milestone in my life. I was confused. I had been stationed at Marine Corps Air Station (MCAS) Tucson, California. The Captain I worked for had assured me that I would not go overseas during my first enlistment because he had talked to the monitor who assigned Aviation Supply Marines. He had been told to allow me to finish my first enlistment at my current duty station because of the important role I played in the organization. But, a year later, here I was at MCAS Futenma in Okinawa, Japan. Luckily, the Captain was also stationed here and I was sure he could help me understand how this had happened.

Once I completed my check-in process, I was now ready to report to the Aviation Supply Department. Now, I would be able to solve this mystery. I checked in with the administrative folks and then made my way to see the Captain since I was told he was going to assign me to my new position. I knocked on his door and he motioned me into his office. I properly reported for assignment and he told me to stand at ease. "Welcome aboard, Sergeant Bernat," he said as he extended his hand to welcome me.

"Thank you, Sir," I replied, "but I am a bit confused. When we were stationed at Tucson, you told me I would not get orders overseas and a year later, here I am overseas. Do you know what happened?"

The Captain laughed. "Sergeant, you did not listen very well. What I said was that as long as I was at Tucson, you did not have to worry about going overseas until your first enlistment was complete. So, let me ask you, where am I now stationed?"

Still puzzled, I replied, "Why, you are here in Okinawa, Sir."

He smiled, "And where are you, now?" A wave of realization washed over me. "That's right. I specifically asked for you to be transferred here after I got here. Sergeant, our keypunch section is awful. They will key in anything you put in front of them and never bother to ensure it is the correct format or information so, as you can guess, most of what goes into the nightly update errors out. I knew I needed a good Sergeant to bring the training and the discipline that it takes to get this section back in line and cut our error rate. And that is when I just knew I needed to get you transferred to Okinawa. So, Sergeant, quit whining and go fix your new section." He gave me directions on how to find the keypunch office and sent me on my way.

Before I tell you what I did to get their attention, let me discuss the important leadership trait of bearing. Bearing is the way in which you conduct and carry yourself. It is vital to making a good first impression. So, always remember:

- **Your manner should reflect alertness, competence, confidence, and control**. When people first meet you, the manner in which you are perceived will set the tone for the future relationship. If the first impression you make demonstrates that you are assured of your abilities and have the capability to accomplish any task you are assigned, you will quickly be seen as an asset and important member of the team. Reflect anything less than these traits and you will spend much of your time building your reputation and having to prove your worth to the organization. The old adage that first impressions count is especially true in business.

- **Hold yourself to the highest standards of personal conduct**. Every day your leadership will be on display to your team. It only takes one misstep to damage everything you have spent years building. Never compromise your values. You can overcome a miscalculation on a report — you will never overcome a loss of your integrity or ethics. Once trust is tarnished, you will never shine again.

- **Never be content with meeting only the minimum requirements**. Anyone can reach the lowest acceptable standards. But if you want to lead your team to excellence, you must demand excellence of yourself. So constantly strive to understand all the functions of your organization and how your function fits into the overall success of the business. Stay on top of current trends in your field of expertise and keep learning all you can about how to take advantage of these. Train yourself and train your team. Most importantly, remember, your example will set the tone for your team so let your bearing shine.

I knew I needed to use my bearing to set the tone for my new team so that they would understand that my arrival meant excellence was going to be the new norm. I walked to the open door of the office and saw three Marines laughing and joking, with their backs to the door. I quietly placed my briefcase down, placed my hands on my hips, and just stared at them. Slowly, one of them turned around and saw me. Instinctively, he quickly jumped to one of the keypunch machines and pretended to work. The other two turned around and then did the same thing. I took one step into the office and said, "The next time I walk into this office, we will start the process of becoming the best keypunch section in the Marine Corps. Pass that on to the night crew Marines. Then prepare yourselves—the fun is about to begin."

Yes, they were full of apprehension—they had no idea what to expect. But they knew immediately that the new Sergeant was about to take them on a wild ride toward excellence and they were either going to get on board or be left behind. In the end, they quickly responded to my training and guidance. Very soon, we were viewed as a valuable asset to the supply operation. And the Captain who requested my transfer to Okinawa told me after the first 30 days that I had lived up to his expectations and then some.

When preparing to take over a new leadership position, remember that your first impression, the manner in which you are perceived on day one, will be so important. So, to be an exceptional leader, use your bearing to announce to the world that outstanding leadership is not just a catch phrase spoken to impress but that it is a way of life for you.

21. Unselfishness

As an Aviation Supply Officer in the Marine Corps, I was in a unique position when we would deploy aboard a naval ship. I was assigned to the helicopter squadron but I also was assigned to the ship's supply department as their S-6 Division Officer. In this capacity, I had both Marines and sailors working for me.

The senior sailor in the division was a Navy chief and since he was the senior enlisted person in the division, he was my assistant to help manage work flow and personnel. When we left the United States, it would take ten days for us to transit to Rota, Spain. There, we would receive an 'in brief' from the squadron that was leaving the Mediterranean theater. On the morning we were arriving in Rota, I was walking across the hangar deck and saw my chief standing near the spot where the gang plank would be placed once we docked. He was in his civilian clothes. So, I walked up beside him and stood for a minute. Then I spoke.

"So, Chief, what are you doing?"

"Getting ready to go ashore once we dock," he replied with a big smile on his face.

"Let me ask you," I inquired with a very icy tone to my voice. "Have you prepared a list of our Marines and sailors who will be going ashore so we know who will be off the ship? Do you know the location of each of their racks so we can check first thing in the morning that they returned safe and sound? Do you know who will be staying on board and have you laid out assignments so they know what you expect for them to accomplish while you are on liberty? Have you done anything that demonstrates to our Marines and sailors that you are here to take care of them during this time we are deployed together?"

"No, Sir, but we don't have to do those things in the Navy," he said swallowing hard.

I smiled. "Chief, you are not working for a Naval Officer. You are working for me. Get below, put on your uniform and take care of your men. Once you have all the information I already laid out, bring your list to me and brief me. Because, in case you haven't figured it out, I will not leave this ship until I know this has been done and that you have left the ship to enjoy liberty. That, Chief, is leadership. You are dismissed. I will see you in our work spaces."

Being a leader means that you must put the welfare of your people ahead of your own desires. This means in every instance, you act unselfishly. Unselfish leadership means:

- **Avoid making yourself comfortable at the expense of others.** In the opening story, the Chief was only thinking of himself. He could not wait to go ashore and enjoy some well-deserved time off. But his people had also earned time to relax and unwind after our ten-day ocean crossing. To have them see the Chief in his civilian clothes ready for liberty while they were still working would have sent them the message that the leadership of this division did not care about them. I had to ensure that perception was squashed immediately. Always put the welfare of your people first. The payback you will receive by having employees who are loyal to you because they know you care for them is priceless.

- **Be considerate of others.** This can be demonstrated in such little things. Hold the door for others, both male and female, to show courtesy. If you drink coffee and have a break room with a coffee pot, offer to get a team member a cup of coffee when you are refilling your cup. Manners count—use please and say thank you often. In other words, let the Golden Rule guide your daily interactions and the bond you build as a team will be priceless.

- **Give credit to those who desire it.** If you really want to show your team that you recognize their efforts, ensure they are properly rewarded. If you have an employee of the month program, make sure you nominate a deserving team member. If a great idea is adopted by the company that was initiated by one of your team members, have the 'big bosses' come and thank them publicly. You should gather your team together and thank them when you successfully complete a project and maybe, have a snack that all can enjoy to celebrate the team's success. Most importantly, never, and I mean never, take credit for an accomplishment of your team or an individual member. Do that but once and you will lose their respect forever. Getting false recognition feels good for a little while but having the undying respect of your team is priceless.

Let me share the last part of the opening story. The next morning, I was gathered with the other Navy Supply Officers for our morning brief. The Ship's Supply Officer told me that the Chief had come to him and complained about my actions the day before. He asked me if it was true that I made the Chief get back in uniform, find out who was leaving the ship and where they slept so we could ensure they returned from liberty, provide instruction to those remaining on board so work continued to be accomplished, and that I would never leave the ship until I received this brief from Chief? I confirmed that I had indeed done just that and I could see the other officers enjoying the fact that "the Marine" was about to be put in his place. To their surprise, the Supply Officer looked at the other officers and said, "I expect each of you to implement the same rules with your division chiefs. We, as the leaders of this department, will ensure we are taking care of our people and watching out for their welfare."

Do you really want to be an exceptional leader? Then be unselfish when it comes to caring for your team and they will become unselfish in their dedication and loyalty to you. And that is priceless.

22. Courage

When we think of courage, we normally associate it with a physical activity where someone is capable of acting despite the fact that physical danger that could lead to injury or death is clearly present. This type of courage is important but there is also another type of courage that should be evident in those in a leadership position... that is moral courage. Let me share a story from my days as a Marine.

I arrived on the island of Okinawa as a Sergeant and took over as the head of the keypunch section. As I discussed my team with the outgoing Corporal, I learned that I had a Lance Corporal working for me who was on a "legal hold" because he had witnessed an assault where three Marines had severely beaten another Marine. He was a government witness and had testified against two of the Marines already but could not say for sure who the third Marine was that was part of the assault. The other two Marines refused to identify the third Marine. So, while waiting for the Navy Criminal Investigative Service (NCIS) to finalize their investigation, he was being held on the island to testify if they could clearly establish the identity of the third Marine. When I arrived, he was already a month past his date to return stateside.

Six months after my arrival, this young Marine came to me in tears. His uncle had died. This uncle had raised him after his parents had been killed in an automobile accident. When he spoke with the legal clerk, he was told that as long as he was on legal hold, he would stay on the island. He went on to tell me that his promotion had also been held up because of the legal hold. He just did not understand. He was not the bad guy; he was there to help the government. The two Marines he had testified against had already completed their sentences and were sent home to the States and he was still stuck on the island. "It just isn't fair, Sergeant Bernat!"

I told him to hold on and went immediately to the Supply Chief, the senior enlisted Marine in our supply department. I explained everything to him and his answer was simple. "This is none of your business. Just go back to work and leave it alone."

Was he kidding? I was stunned by his lack of concern for one of his Marines. So, I went to my office, put on my cover, and went right to the headquarters to speak with the command Sergeant Major, our senior enlisted Marine in the entire command. Luckily, he was in his office so I politely knocked and requested permission to speak to him concerning a very important matter. He invited me in and I proceeded to outline what my Marine had told me. When I was done, he yelled at the top of his voice for the senior legal clerk to get to his office. The Gunnery Sergeant from legal immediately appeared with a surprised look on his face.

"Gunny, bring me the paperwork concerning the legal hold of Lance Corporal Smith (not his real name)."

"Uh…well, Sergeant Major," the Gunny stammered, "there

really is no paperwork on his legal hold. NCIS had told us to hold him until 'his memory improved and he named the third Marine in the assault' since they could not obtain enough evidence to charge anyone else."

The Sergeant Major smiled at me. "Thanks, Sergeant Bernat, for bringing this to my attention. I will take it from here. You are dismissed and close the door on the way out."

I don't know why he had me close the door. Everyone heard what he was saying and it was very clear that he was not happy.

As a leader, there will be times when you are faced with the difficult decision to do what is right or to just go along with a broken system. Moral courage means that in every case, you must stand up and do the right thing. Here are the benefits you will reap that make tilting at windmills worth the difficulties you may face.

- Your team will see that you are willing to stand firm to ensure that each person is treated with the dignity and respect they deserve. The end result will be that you will have their complete loyalty—and that is priceless.

- For your team members, you will be a role model of courageous leadership and when they are faced with a situation where they have to choose between doing what is right or not, they will remember your courage and hopefully do what is right.

- Most importantly, you will be able to look at yourself in the mirror each day and know that your ethical and moral compass is truly aligned in the right direction.

If you do what is right will that make you popular? I would love to tell you that you will receive accolades for fighting on the side of right but my own experiences have taught me that in most cases, you will be considered a trouble maker; a problem that needs to be eliminated. But do it anyway. Let me finish the story I started and you will see what I mean.

Shortly after talking to the Sergeant Major, my lance corporal was called to the Commanding Officer's office and was promoted to corporal with his original promotion date and all back pay and allowances. Arrangements were made to get him home as quickly as possible so he could be there with his aunt for the funeral. He was to check in with the local recruiter's office until new orders were issued for his next duty assignment stateside so he would not have to return overseas. I was so happy for my Marine and wished him well as he hurried back to the barracks to get packed up for his return home.

Of course, the Supply Chief called me to his office and he was not too happy with me. "Why did you go over my head after I told you to leave it alone? What do you have to say for yourself?"

I looked at his angry face and could not help but smile. "I did it because it was the right thing to do. And I would do it again, if necessary."

To be an exceptional leader, you have to have the courage to take a stand and do the right thing—not sometimes, but every time. Be an exceptional leader.

23. Knowledge

I was a young Sergeant working later than normal and I noticed that the Gunnery Sergeant in the Stock Control Section was also still at work. He had a look on his face that told me something was bothering him. I approached his desk and asked, "Is everything okay, Gunny?"

"I was just looking at my LES (leave and earnings statement—the military equivalent of a pay stub). The end of the fiscal year is coming up and I am about to lose another 30 days of leave."

I did some quick figuring in my head. In the Marine Corps, we earned 30 days of leave a year. We could keep up to 60 days of leave on the books at the end of a fiscal year. To lose 30 days, you have to go three years without taking any leave. To "lose another 30 days of leave" means the Gunny had not taken any leave in at least four years!

"Gunny, why haven't you taken leave in so long?" I asked with a tone of shock in my voice.

"Well, Sergeant, if I take so much as a week of leave, I spend the next two to three weeks correcting everything that was done wrong while I was out. No, I just can't afford to take time off. Without me, this place would not function."

Now, this is where I showed just how naive I was. I asked what I thought was a good question. "Well, Gunny, why don't you train your people to do their jobs so that you don't have to fix things when you get back?"

To clean up his response, he told me to stick to my pay grade, not to speak to him anymore, and to quickly exit from his sight.

Too many people in a position of leadership feel that it is important that they keep important knowledge from their team so that they are able to maintain control over their team. They create within themselves an air of importance because "everyone must come to me for answers because only I know the big picture." Most important to this kind of leader is they believe their boss will see them as pivotal to the operation. However, they miss these important downsides to this kind of attitude.

- Keeping important information from your team does not make you important; it makes you selfish. Eventually, your team will realize you withhold information to increase your own sense of importance and to maintain control over them. Slowly but surely, they will lose their respect for you and begin to look for other opportunities. Your personnel turnover rate will be a problem.

- You are creating an information dam where you dole out just enough information to allow your team to move to the next step but not enough information to allow them to think on their own and come up with new and innovative solutions. You are stifling the creativity that could earn your team recognition for process improvement or cost savings. Your good folks will be frustrated and try to learn more. If you continue to hold them back, you will lose your most important asset—your good team members. In the end, you will have a team of people who have no self-motivation and only do what you tell them to do.

- You will put work before family because you cannot risk allowing your team to be successful without you. If you are not there, how will the bosses know you were the driving factor to bring about the success? In the end, you will risk losing your family just to maintain this false impression that you are indispensable at work.

- You will never get the promotion you desire. Why? Because you will have been successful in convincing your boss that your team cannot function without you and you will be stuck in the same job.

Thanks to this important conversation with the Gunny, I was able to create my "Three-Day Rule" and I have lived by this ever since. This rule, when properly applied, will ensure success for both your team and you, create a bond of oneness within your team, prove to your team you are dedicated to their advancement and success, and prepare you to move up the corporate ladder as a proven leader. Here is my rule.

"I will train my team members so well, that should I die while sitting at my desk, it will be three days before anyone

notices I am dead. Most importantly, they will not notice I am dead because the job is not being done. They will notice I am dead because I will begin to stink."

If you want to be an exceptional leader, start by instituting the Three-Day Rule. Ensure you train your team — teach them everything you know — help them grow and succeed. Trust me when I say, it pays dividends.

24. Loyalty

As the executive officer (XO) of a Marine training command, I had just finished going over the Fitness Report (civilian equivalent of an evaluation) with my administrative officer. I was pleased that I could grade him outstanding (the highest possible grade) on most areas of the evaluation. There were four areas where I felt improvement was possible and I had graded him as excellent in these areas (the second highest grade possible). I had outlined my reason for each mark and provided a positive improvement program that would ensure his next evaluation would contain all outstanding grades. His reaction floored me.

"No, Sir," he said, "I always get all outstanding marks. You will not like what happens if you do not give me all outstanding marks."

"Warrant Officer, are you threatening me?" I asked firmly.

"No, Sir, I am just telling you that you need to change this or you will regret it," he replied.

"The Fitness Report will be submitted as written, Warrant Officer. You are dismissed."

By that afternoon, the Warrant Officer handed me my copy of a letter he had sent outlining why my evaluation of his performance was tainted by my obvious racial discrimination against black Marines. He had sent the letter to the President of the United States, the Secretary of Defense, both the Congressman and Senator of the district in the State of Mississippi where we were stationed, the Chief of Naval Operations, the Commandant of the Marine Corps, the Commanding General of the Marine Corps Education and Training Command, the Chief of Naval Training, the Chief of Naval Technical Training, the Commanding Officer of the Naval Technical Training Center, and finally, our commanding officer (who was now implicated by the fact that "he had allowed it"). Before it was all settled, he would send several more of these shot gun letters out concerning how he felt I was retaliating against him for making this information known. As a result, there was an in-depth investigation into my leadership and how I evaluated my Marines that would take a toll on the command, my Marines, my wife, and of course, me.

As soon as I realized what was about to happen (I knew based upon the letter that once someone figured out who was responsible for actually looking into this matter, an investigation would be coming), I went to my commanding officer. I instructed him that because of this letter, he needed to counsel me on my responsibility as a Marine Officer to be fair and impartial in the treatment of my Marines and in their evaluations. I told him the documentation he was to create to cover this counseling must state in no uncertain terms that the Marine Corps, the command, and he personally would not tolerate racial discrimination in any form. I made it clear that whatever he put in writing, I would sign without question.

"Why? Why would you tell me to do this, XO?"

"Sir," I began, "I know that I have done nothing wrong but sometimes, that is not always important in an investigation of this nature. I have 18 years in the Corps. Whatever happens as a result of this investigation, I will be allowed to finish my last two years and retire. I may be in some out of the way place, but I will get my 20. However, you are a young officer and have a long, promising career ahead of you. You need to do this to ensure that when the investigation starts, you can demonstrate that you took immediate action to ensure your command was not going to tolerate any form of discrimination."

"But, XO, if you have done nothing wrong, why are you telling to counsel you?" The CO was still bewildered by my request. I had a one-word answer for him.

"Loyalty."

Loyalty means that you are devoted to the company for whom you work, to the leadership of your company, to your peers, and to your team members. But for loyalty to be an asset that creates success, we need to understand every aspect of this trait.

- Loyalty is not something you insist upon, it is something you earn. Any discussion of this trait must begin with this very important understanding.

- Loyalty is a two-way street. You have to show loyalty in every aspect of your performance but the organization, the leadership, your peers, and your team must also be loyal to you.

- Loyalty is not an excuse to compromise your integrity. As a matter of fact, any leader who would ask you to compromise your values or the values established by the company for the sake of loyalty is not being loyal to you.

- Loyalty does not take advantage of your loyalty. We all have families and need to have ample time to be with them. We all need time away from work to relieve the stress of our jobs. We all need rest to enable us to have the energy to devote to our jobs. So, if your leaders are constantly asking for more and more of your time and using "as a loyal employee" for justification, they have stopped caring for you and are now taking advantage of you.

- All organizations have problems but loyalty says you keep them internal. Do not discuss the problems in your company with others — especially your competition.

- Being loyal to the leadership of your organization means you never talk bad about the leaders in your company to subordinates. If you disagree with one of your bosses, go to him or her and discuss it so that you can present a united front to your team,

- Which brings us to the last important aspect of loyalty; you may not always agree with the decisions that come from the front office, but if the instructions are not a violation of your integrity or the law, you have an obligation to support and implement the new policy as if you had come up with the idea yourself.

So, after many months of investigation and over 400 pages of verbatim testimony, I was exonerated of all accusations. It turned out that the Warrant Officer had used this threat every time a reporting senior had pointed out a deficiency. In the past, it had always worked in that they would give him the grades he wanted. He was shocked that I just would not give into his demand. As he told the investigator, it would have been so easy if I had just given him all outstanding marks like he wanted.

And my CO. He told me as he was leaving and turning the command over to me that he knew it was in good hands because he had never met a more loyal Marine who was willing to do whatever was necessary to protect the Corps, the Command, and his fellow Marines.

To be recognized as an exceptional leader, you must demonstrate uncompromising loyalty.

25. Endurance

In the summer of 1972, Hurricane Agnes came through the state of Pennsylvania. I was 17 at the time and was a volunteer fireman and state certified Emergency Medical Technician (EMT) with Fame Fire Company #2 in Lewistown. I believe it was a Sunday at about 9:00 am when the fire alarms sounded and I immediately ran to the firehouse, just a half block from where I lived. Our captain was standing in the doorway of the radio room and was getting everyone to gather in front of him as they arrived. Once he felt all who were going to respond to the alarm had arrived, he began to address us.

"We have received word that the rivers and creeks in our area are about to overflow their banks and because the rain is going to continue for several more hours, the flooding is going to be extremely bad. I need to know who can stay here at the firehouse to be ready to respond to emergency rescues, fire calls, and medical emergencies. We will probably have to remain in the station for at least a couple of days."

Once he had his volunteers, he sent the rest of the responders who could not stay home and began to make assignments. Since I was a certified EMT, I was assigned to the first run ambulance for medical emergencies. Little did I know just how difficult this assignment was going to be and how it would test the very limits of my endurance.

Endurance is the mental and physical stamina that is measured by your ability to withstand pain, fatigue, stress, and hardship. We will all be faced with times in our lives when we will have to be able to go above and beyond — to dig deep within our emotional strength to enable us to keep our thinking clear and to tap into our physical strength to move forward when we just want to quit. You will never know when a situation in life will present itself and force you to tap into your ability to endure, but you can prepare yourself so that when the time comes, you will be ready. Here are some tips.

- **Eat well**. In the hustle and bustle of everyday life, we may have a tendency to skip meals, eat fast food on the go, and snack on sweets or gulp energy drinks/coffee to give us a short burst of energy. But our bodies work more efficiently if we eat a balanced diet. So, do some research, attend a class or seminar on nutrition, talk to your doctor, or have a discussion with your personal trainer, but create a diet that will meet your personal needs while providing you all the necessary nutrition to allow your body to function at its peak performance at all times.

- **Exercise**. When you are called to exhibit strong endurance, having yourself in good physical shape will enable you to keep going even when your body screams stop. Exercise will help you to build this type of stamina because you will have taught yourself to work through the exhaustion and pain to keep going. Of course, if you are about to start an exercise program for the first time or after a long layoff from such activity, please see your doctor for a complete physical so that you can ensure yourself that you have no underlying health issues that need to be considered before creating a program. If you are not sure how to get started or what to do, find a personal trainer who can guide you based on your medical and health factors.

- **Learn to control stress**. There are different breathing techniques and meditation techniques that allow you to manage high levels of stress very quickly. Try closing your eyes and picturing a calm scene. Now inhale slowly through your nose and then slowly exhale through your mouth. In a minute or two, you will be surprised at how your stress has been reduced and you will be able to once again get your mind to function at its peak of performance. If you need other techniques, visit your local yoga studio for some tips.

- **Practice**. To build your confidence, look for assignments that will require you to work a little harder than normal and will test your ability to endure while under stress. This can be done by starting that project your spouse has been asking you to do for some time, heading up a committee at your place of worship, volunteering with one of the many organizations that need folks every day to roll up their sleeves and just provide physical labor to succeed, or taking on a new role at work that will require you to pursue new and exciting opportunities to learn and grow. No matter what manner you choose, finish every task to the best of your ability by forcing yourself to continue when you are physically tired and your mind is sluggish.

Here is how I learned these valuable lessons in endurance. I was so glad I was 17 at the time and in good enough shape to endure the challenge.

Once the flooding starting in our little town, it did not take long for the north side of town to be completely cut off from the south side of town. Our sister station with ambulance service on the south side of town could not get to the hospital. We worked with the State Police and found out that there was one spot along the by-pass that went around the town that would allow them to bring their patient into a subdivision on the south end of town next to the bypass. We would park on the shoulder of the by-pass and they would carry their patient on a backboard across a lawn and hand them over the guard rail to the driver and me. We would then place the backboard on the litter and load the patient into our ambulance. Carefully, the driver would drive across the grass median and head for the hospital while I attended to the patient's needs. The next time we had to pick up a patient from them, we would give them their backboard and they would load up the next patient. Between emergencies to which we responded and emergencies where we had to meet the other ambulance team to transfer a patient, I was awake and responding to calls for 72 hours straight (For safety purposes, the drivers were swapped out but our limitation on EMT's keep me in the ambulance non-stop). I had to help with rescues, administer first aid to those in my care, and even perform CPR for 40 minutes in the back of the ambulance while the driver maneuvered the back roads and side streets to get around the flooding so we could get to the hospital. By the time I finally was able to stop and rest, I had pushed myself to the very end of my endurance. However, I had taken care of each person to the very best of my ability. I was tired and my muscles ached but I was grateful that I was able to help our town in this important time when the need was overwhelming for many.

If you are going to be an exceptional leader, prepare yourself, both mentally and physically, to work through stress, pain, and exhaustion to demonstrate endurance during emergency situations.

Part 3: Final Words

26. Bringing It All Together

I have now shared with you eleven leadership principles and fourteen traits of a leader that I learned while serving in the Marine Corps. These principles helped me lead my Marines in difficult situations and helped me be successful in my career outside the Marine Corps. Let me give you my most challenging experience and see if you can come up with the same solutions I did.

I was selected to head a test project. An existing division in the Aviation Supply Department would have its mission changed to become an internal audit division working directly for the Supply Officer. This division would be the eyes and ears of the Supply Officer to ensure the Assistant Supply Officer was operating the supply department according to the established Marine Corps orders. This was a dramatic change since in the past, all divisions worked and answered to the Assistant Supply Officer with no one holding this position accountable for operational decisions.

The Assistant Supply Officer for whom I was working was very upset. He did not like the idea that in this new position, I could report problems I found directly to the Supply Officer without ever discussing the problem with him. I assured him that any officer that would use this position as a "got you" against another officer would not be able to effectively do this job because of the internal strife it would cause in the supply department. He was not buying it and he made it clear he was not going to support this test.

Since higher headquarters had insisted I be the officer heading up the test, the Assistant Supply Officer had no say in my assignment. But, he would have to provide me with the Marines who would be working for me during the test period. On the morning we began the implementation of the test project, my fellow Captain called me to his office and told me that my team was being assembled and taken to the office space we would be using. With a smile that can only be described as evil, he said, "Good luck making this test work." With a chuckle, he dismissed me.

When I went to my office area, here is the team he had provided me. A Vietnam veteran Master Sergeant with a bullet still lodged in his back who the Captain was trying desperately to have discharged for medical reasons since he could not run (the fear being the bullet might shift and paralyze him). As you can guess, the Master Sergeant was no fan of the Captain. A Gunnery Sergeant charged with molesting his step-daughter and facing a General Court Martial who would be spending a lot of time at the base legal office. A Staff Sergeant with lymphoma who spent much of his time at medical appointments and a Staff Sergeant charged with negligent homicide, also busy with his legal team. Finally, my team was rounded out with a Corporal facing a General Court Martial for raping a 16-year-old girl and two Lance Corporals facing charges for selling drugs.

As I stood there, I knew I had to come up with the right words to ensure I immediately had this team ready to go to work in spite of everything else that was going on in their lives. So, I ask you. What would you have said to ensure you could successfully test this important change that everyone from Washington DC to the local command was watching and expecting a fair and accurate assessment of an internal auditing division?

Before I tell you what I said on that very challenging day, let me remind you of the leadership principles that I have been discussing that would provide the best solution to this very precarious situation.

If you are going to lead, you need to start by looking inward and assessing yourself. You need to prepare yourself for leadership by following some very specific principles that will ensure your team, no matter how diverse, will follow you in the most difficult of situations. These five principles are necessary if you expect to be a successful leader.

- Know yourself and seek self-improvement

- Be technically proficient

- Seek responsibility and take responsibility for your actions

- Make sound and timely decisions

- Set the example

Once you have worked on preparing yourself for a leadership position, then you need to remember these six principles that will help you lead a winning team; a team that works together to be successful.

- Know your employees and look out for their welfare

- Develop a sense of responsibility among your employees

- Keep your employees informed

- Ensure assigned tasks are understood, supervised, and accomplished

- Train your team

- Employ your team in accordance with its capabilities

Have you thought about what you would have done when faced with the team members that the good Captain had provided me? Here is what I said and how I handled these Marines.

"Gentleman, each of you faces a time in your life where, whether you know it or not, you will be looking to me for help. Whether you are facing a medical review board or a jury of your peers, I will be called upon to testify as to your value as a Marine and your potential in the future as a Marine or in the civilian world. I hold the keys to your discharge or punishment; I can make a difference in your future. It is my desire that I can make a positive difference in your life (***principle - Know your employees and look out for their welfare***)."

"But, what happens is completely up to you. If you give 100% to me as we test this vital function in the supply department (*principle - Develop a sense of responsibility among your employees*), I will give 100% to you when I am called to testify on your behalf and believe me, you will know exactly what to expect when I take the stand because I will have let you know if I believe you gave me your all (*principle - Keep your employees informed*)."

After that, we rolled up our sleeves and got to work. I reviewed each inspection checklist before we went into any division (*principle - Ensure assigned tasks are understood, supervised, and accomplished*), conducted training on how to investigate each inspection requirement and answered their questions so that they were prepared to conduct each audit (*principle - Train your team*). Finally, I assigned each task based on my reading of their understanding of the task that we were about to undertake (*principle - Employ your team in accordance with its capabilities*).

What about my fellow Captain? After each division audit, I sat down with him and briefed him on our findings (*principle — Know yourself and seek self-improvement*). When problems were discovered, we formulated a plan of action to correct the problem and implemented the plan together (*principles - Be technically proficient; Seek responsibility and take responsibility for your actions*). Finally, we briefed the Supply Officer on what **we** found and how **we** had corrected the problem (*principle — make sound and timely decisions*). Together, the Captain and I formulated local training that needed to be conducted at all levels of the organization to improve our effectiveness as a combat aviation supply department (*principle—Set the example*). In other words, to his amazement, the Captain realized the new audit division was necessary and paid great dividends when teamwork was the end goal.

When the final brief was made to all the higher commands, the recommendation was that this would be a vital and necessary change that would improve combat readiness within the Marine aviation community.

The principles I have shared will make you the kind of leader you have always wanted to be and will help you be the kind of leader your people have always wanted you to be. Be an exceptional leader—lead with these leadership principles and traits in mind.

Acknowledgements

Every dream becomes a reality because of a team of individuals who work behind the scenes to add their support and talent to help turn a vision into an accomplishment. I would like to thank the following folks who were part of my journey.

My wife, Hazel, who is a constant source of encouragement. She supported me from my early days as a Marine Officer, through the difficult transition to civilian life, as I answered the surprise calling to become an ordained minister, and now, as I use this final retirement from the workforce to become an author and lecturer on leadership. Her love for me and her belief in my abilities made it possible for me to face each day with the knowledge that no matter what happened, she would always stand with me. Hazel, you have my undying love.

I can't help but thank Dennis Pitocco, the creator of the awarding winning website Bizcatalyst360.com, who offered me a forum to share my articles on leadership with his worldwide audience. Because of the encouragement I received from Dennis and the comments I received from my articles, this book began to take shape.

Thanks to Christine Andola who shared her experiences with

the publishing of her first book. Her insights helped me avoid the many pitfalls that first-time authors face and allowed me to select a publisher who understood my vision and how to approach this project as a team dedicated to success. Christine, I will always consider you friendship a gift of immeasurable value.

And of course, so much credit belongs to Bob Babcock, Jan Babcock, Mark Babcock, Matt King and the rest of the team at Deeds Publishing. From the very first meeting with Bob, I instantly knew that I had found a group of people who would work tirelessly to help me bring this book from my computer to a readership that was seeking to not just be a good leader but to grow into an exemplary leader. The professionalism, experience, guidance, and encouragement I received allowed me to take my 'ugly baby' and clean it up so that today, I am proud to share my 'baby' with you.

About the Author

Len Bernat is a leader groomed by 20 years of molding and shaping by some of the finest leaders in the United States Marine Corps. Their guidance helped Len realize his full potential as he moved from an enlisted Marine to becoming an Officer of Marines. Len became known for being the leader who could turn any lackluster organization into a strong, functional unit. Upon his retirement, Len worked in several positions before finally starting a second career in governmental procurement. His experience and leadership skills enabled him to be recognized as the 2011 Governmental Procurement Officer of the Year for the Governmental Procurement Association of Georgia and opened doors for him to teach at many of the association's conferences. Len was also called to the ministry and was ordained at Ashford Memorial Methodist Church in November of 1999. Today, Len is the Pastor of Maxeys Christian Church in Maxeys, Georgia. Len has been married to his wife, Hazel, for 36 years and they have three daughters, three grandchildren, and three great-grandchildren

CPSIA information can be obtained
at www.ICGtesting.com
Printed in the USA
FFOW03n2028031217
43868134-42849FF